Always trust all your heart. And know I was raped by family and a farm hand when I was five and my mother didn't believe me and it caused hatred for years in my life. I never did drugs + Alchol, but I have a hard time with relationships. But God Blessed me with a wonderful family + husband. Don't think you are worthless cause God is bigger than all the worries + troubles we have. Trust God & believe His promise is true. Take time out for Jesus and pray + read your bible + he will lead you wherever you go.

Desperate for a Fix

*If You Only Knew How
One Good Decision
Could Change Your Life*

By: Dana M. Brown

Published on July 27, 2016
Copyright © 2016 Dana M. Brown.
All Rights Reserved.

I would like to dedicate this book my Mom and Dad, Bill Burns and Bill Foley, without you all I may not have made it to share this story.

To my sister, Selena, my family and friends; all of you who prayed for me while
I was a hot mess. Praying against hope, thinking I may be too far gone.

To the maintenance man on Avenue B, thank you for your kindness.

To Pastor Paul Brafford for giving me a chance and being my mentor for all those early years. You are amazing.

I would also like to dedicate this book to all of the people who have made really bad decisions, who struggle to forgive themselves, and live everyday feeling like that part of your life is a big black hole of darkness. Keep in mind, your life WILL unfold and you have a say in how that happens. Make that darkness a bright light of hope for someone else. Find Peace and run with it.

Last but not least, I dedicate this book to God, our kids:
Chad Brown, Che' Brown,
Alyssa Guckert, Lance Brown, Jaden Brown,
and to my husband Mark Brown.
You all drive me crazy, but keep me sane.

Table of Contents

Foreword	*Dr. Bill Wilson*
Chapter 1	*How Did I Get Here*
Chapter 2	*Rape*
Chapter 3	*Filling the Void*
Chapter 4	*It Should Have Been the Most Difficult Decision of My Life*
Chapter 5	*Add Money to the Equation*
Chapter 6	*My First Arrest*
Chapter 7	*No Regrets-Big Apple Bound*
Chapter 8	*Building My Castle*
Chapter 9	*My First True Love*
Chapter 10	*Prostitution*
Chapter 11	*Homelessness*
Chapter 12	*Someone Is Killing Prostitutes on the Lower East Side*
Chapter 13	*The Kindness of a Stranger*
Chapter 14	*Lost Gift, Found Heartache*
Chapter 15	*I Am a Felon*
Chapter 16	*Courthouse Chaos*
Chapter 17	*My Two Bills*
Chapter 18	*DayTop*
Chapter 19	*Good Things Happen to Good People*
Chapter 20	*The Cycle Continues*
Chapter 21	*My Non-Heroic Account of September 11, 2001*
Chapter 22	*The Beginning of Change*
Chapter 23	*A New Life*
Chapter 24	*Interview/Counseling Session*
Chapter 25	*How Great Is My God*
Chapter 26	*Trouble in Paradise*
Chapter 27	*The Luxury Apartments*
Chapter 28	*A New Home for a New Start*
Chapter 29	*The Desires of My Heart*
Afterword	

Foreword

Through the 35+ years that I have lived here and worked in the inner city of New York, there has been a segment of society -- the homeless, the prostitutes, the drug addicts, that I have ministered to with a peculiar curiosity.

When I look at some of the people we've worked with and try to understand why they chose to live the way they have, I've had to ask myself some pretty intense questions. Why build a friendship knowing that more than likely many of these people would end up dead? To become a glutton for punishment? There's a reason why.

There was one girl that we worked with – her name was Angel. Between the prostitution and the crack habit, she was simply a classic example of urban hopelessness. Somehow if anyone, I thought had a chance to beat the odds and get out of this hellhole of what her life had become, it was Angel. She just didn't seem to belong on the gritty streets of Brooklyn. It was a long journey getting her out of the area and sending her into rehabs, more than once, countless hours of my staff working with her, getting her into church. She was clean and she stuck to it for a while, attending church faithfully. I really thought she would even come on staff one day. Fifteen years of working with Angel – my last "mission" for her was performing her funeral. I don't know if she just didn't get "it," or that she could not conquer those demons or just lost the "want to." I wish I could have read her mind.

Dana's story is a first-hand account of what motivates a

person to make the choices they've made to fall into the throngs of homelessness, of prostitution, of drug abuse. And what it takes to connect with folks on their level.

I dare you to read this with the intent of not only increasing your comprehension but more importantly, expanding your own capacity to look upon those who live in this darkness with a deeper sense of compassion and patience, and be willing to say, "whatever it takes!"

Bill Wilson, Senior Pastor & Founder
Metro Ministries
Author of *Whose Child is This?* and *In the Crosshairs*
Producer of Documentaries *Streets of Pain* and *Gone Before Dawn*

Chapter One
How Did I Get Here?

I regained consciousness on a putrid, old couch from a heroin induced nap, or "nod" as we junkies called it. The night before, I injected an extremely potent shot that caused warmth to permeate my body. Immediately, I drifted off into a semi-conscious state and all my cares disappeared into the darkness. It was the closest thing to heaven I could possibly imagine at the time. It was the only time I felt peace.

On that particular day, I was exhausted because sleep had eluded me for several nights. I hadn't been in the room long enough to remember much about it. All I recall is I was in a strange, dark bedroom with a sofa, and a TV on but muted. I looked over to the bed and saw him lying there face down. Thinking back to the night before, I barely remembered meeting him when he pulled up beside me on the street. He held up a bag of dope and asked if I wanted to party. I never turned down free drugs, especially heroin.

The dope was a master at not allowing me to consider the danger of climbing into a car with a man I didn't know. I honestly didn't care what might happen. The potential to make money or get high was at hand and that was motivation enough for me. I blocked out any hint of intuition that told me it was a bad idea.

We headed back to his place, not saying much of anything along the way. I'm sure we made the regular small talk, all of which was unimportant and quite honestly, very unnecessary. Neither of us truly cared who or what the other was or did. Upon arrival, we quickly prepared our drugs and took the heroin. I shot mine up, while he sniffed his. I must have immediately nodded out because I don't remember anything until the moment I woke up on the couch. I know we didn't have sex, because when I rose, I was still dressed and so was he. I don't think I even knew his name. But that was normal; I rarely knew the names of the men I did business with.

Stumbling over to the bed, still high from the dope, I said, "Hey, get up. I gotta go!"

I didn't know where I had to go. All I knew is that I just wanted to get out of there. If we didn't have sex, then he wasn't going to pay me and all the drugs seemed to be gone, so there was no reason for me to stick around.

I yelled again. Nothing.

"Hey!" I said louder as I leaned over and shoved him a little. It was cold in the room, and he felt cold as well. Although it was still dark, when I rolled him over, I could see he had a purple tint on his face. I snatched my hand back and my breath left me for a few seconds.

From the corner of my eyes I could see colors streak and run together from the TV, blinking its light into the room. It reminded me of a horror movie and at any moment the killer would jump out from behind a door or piece of furniture. My mind raced with the situation, the truth of what my life had become and the darkness I was living in.

Am I dreaming? Is this real?

In my drugged condition, it was difficult to comprehend what I was seeing. The denial that the drugs allowed entered once again. It helped me cope through so many situations that without it I may have lost my mind completely. Reality was something I didn't contend with very well. I took great steps to escape it. The main step was using drugs. All steps included drugs.

Sometimes after shooting up and getting on the train, I'd drift off into a nod so soundly that I would miss my subway stops. Other times, if I was eating, I would nod right off into my food. I had done this several times in various dives, which was just as embarrassing as if it occurred at a five-star restaurant. But, thankfully the drugs would whisk away the humiliation and I could continue in my denial. Any normal person might learn their lesson from such situations, but not a junkie. The drugs convinced us that no one noticed. And who cares if they did notice. But at this moment it could eliminate the current catastrophe I found myself in; at least in my mind and I desperately needed a fix.

I couldn't bring myself to check his pulse or touch his skin. I had never seen a dead man before, much less been alone in the same room with one. I tried to convince myself that he merely passed out. But I knew in my heart he was dead. Reality crept back into my mind and my heart sank down to my gut as the certainty of it hit me and I panicked. It was quiet in the room and I could hear my own breath, my heart pounded like a drum, and every noise outside on the street echoed throughout my body, lingering until the noises competed for my mind's attention.

I don't know how long I had been nodded out, but the sun was just beginning to rise. The shades were drawn, however a faint light peered into the room illuminating the dust particles flying in the air. His silhouette was outlined in the dim light as I began to back away from the bed.

Don't throw up. Just get outta here. Where the hell am I?

I checked my purse, "Damn, no money," I stated out loud, as if he could do anything about it. I don't know why it was such a shock; I never had any extra money. As soon as I got it, I immediately spent it. If I had ten dollars, I bought drugs, if I had a dollar, I bought cookies or some sort of junk food. I had a talent for being able to spend every cent I had. A nickel would buy me a piece of candy or gum. I could work it down to the penny with tax and leave with zero.

I carried all my worldly possessions in that little bag. It seems hard to believe that a person could carry all of their belongings in a pocket book. But I had to keep it that way. I didn't have a home and as a prostitute, I simply couldn't push a cart around. No john would allow you to carry a bunch of stuff into his car. I had to travel light. One might think that in New York City, you could find millions of places to hide your stuff. But most of the time, someone else had already found that spot and if their own stuff wasn't there, they would steal your belongings if you decided to leave them there. No, I had to travel light.

I looked again over at the bed and saw the bump in his back pocket. *His wallet.* I went back into escape mode, where I could ignore what I was getting ready to do. I walked back over to the bed, pushed him a little to access the pocket and took out his wallet. As I looked inside I thought *"Thank God"* to a God that I didn't even believe existed. I grabbed the small stack of cash inside, threw the wallet on the bed and sprinted for the door with the unrealistic hope that all of this would go away as soon as I got to my dealer.

Once outside the apartment, the sun was getting brighter and higher in the sky. I was momentarily relieved, breathing out a giant sigh. But now, a new anxiety overtook my thoughts.

I need to get to my dealer in Manhattan and get some drugs. But, where am I? I must be in one of the Burroughs. This is not the city. God, I hope it doesn't take too long to get there. I was so immensely afraid of accepting the truth that I would have anxiety attacks. These attacks made me believe I would die if I had to deal with situations without the assistance of my drugs.

As I tried to figure out a way to get back to the city, more thoughts assailed me.

How did you get here, Dana? How did you get to this point in your life? What happened? Where did you go wrong? This is not how you should be.

I tried my best to ignore these latest thoughts. Reality scared me and only brought me pain. My life had never been very warm and fuzzy. First, I was a difficult child and my adolescence was hard, all stemming from my own insecurities and rebellion. Now, the current brutal truth hit me. I was a homeless prostitute, addicted to heroin and cocaine, and I had found myself in a room with a man I believed to be dead. Plus, I had zero self-esteem. Zero. The only value I understood was the amount of money a man would pay for "me." I was at the lowest point in my life, and the only way I could survive was to avoid reality; and that needed to happen as soon as possible.

Finally, the restlessness and nagging of needing to self-medicate took over again. I required an escape. I started walking down the street, not knowing where I was going, just going. Fortunately, a gypsy cab came and stopped as I waved it down. Gypsy cabs were usually un-metered and unregulated cabs that were run by people trying to make some extra money. I understood that concept and it didn't bother me at all.

All I could muster to say to the driver was, "9th Street and Avenue C, Manhattan." I could hardly wait to get to my cocaine dealer's spot and feel that rush of relief I always got from shooting coke. I alternated between cocaine and heroin. If I experienced heroin withdrawal, I would buy heroin. If not, I bought cocaine. Cocaine allowed me to stay up and active, which is necessary when you live on the streets and need to be ready for any opportunity to make money or need to get out of danger.

I curled up on the back seat of the cab to avoid looking at the driver. I was very withdrawn when it came to normal everyday things like riding in a cab or the subway, but when it came to making money, this alter-ego protruded from my personality and allowed me to be someone else. Someone that could sleep with men she didn't know for money and someone who could take money from a dead man's wallet.

I noticed the cab smelled like armpit, but I wasn't sure if it was the driver or me. I hadn't showered in a couple of days and felt sure he hadn't either. It was a toss-up of who the odor was coming from.

Having a shower was a luxury for me and many other street people. Most of us just stopped trying to find a place to shower and became used to our own smell. Occasionally I could shower at a john's house or at the hotel where we did our business, but most of the time, we were in a car. A few johns would put me up in hotels and buy me clothes, but not many and not very often. But, even when they did, the clothes would eventually be lost to the city out of need to find something cleaner to wear. I didn't own a toothbrush or a hairbrush. I wore whatever I could find that someone had thrown out. My clothes never fit and sometimes they weren't even women's clothes. They were always dirty, some worse than others. I was always dirty. A homeless prostitute certainly isn't glamorous. No prostitute is glamorous. It is actually a pretty pathetic, demeaning life, and so hard to escape. Despite my multiple attempts.

I found the battle with myself, in my mind, to be futile. It didn't matter what I wanted to happen. And when I tried to crawl out of the hole I was in, my addiction would seize all thoughts and refocus my mind on getting more drugs. So, in order to have any peace, I gave in to its control.

I felt sick to my stomach and tried to focus on getting more drugs and not the harshness of what I just left back in the apartment. But, reality consumed my mind again. In a fetal position on the backseat, I covered my face with my arms and sobbed all the way to the corner bodega. There I could get something to numb the emotions I was feeling. After what seemed like an eternity, we arrived at the little store, my bodega, my haven.

I threw $40 over the seat, hoping it was enough, and jumped out of the cab. I wasn't as cautious as I usually was when going to buy drugs. Most of the time, I would get dropped off around the corner and look down the streets and on the roof tops before going into the store, but this time I got out right in front and went straight in. I was desperate, more so than usual, and I thought I would expire if I didn't get something to numb the hurt I was feeling.

Inside the musty old store was a small counter immediately to the left. On it were clear plastic bins filled with bite-sized candies. All different types, Butterfinger, Milky Way, Gobstoppers, but the Now and Laters were my favorite. The sweets were probably the only food items in the store that anyone ever purchased. Once past the counter, there were about four isles of convenient mart style foods, cans of pork-n-beans, boxes of Hamburger Helper, Vienna Sausages. All of it was covered in a layer of dust you could write your name in. No one bought food there, just cocaine and candy.

I was relieved to see that my favorite dealer was there behind the counter. He was a neatly trimmed Dominican, always wearing gold necklaces or gold bracelets, and had a flair for fashion. Most of the Dominicans I knew did, they prided themselves on looking good. He was always friendly to me. He smiled when I came in and never looked down at me like most of the dealers on the streets. He made me feel like he liked me, although I knew he didn't. We could never be real friends. But, at that moment, he was the only thing close to a friend that I had. I knew I could tell him anything and he wouldn't share it with anyone. He kept secrets. So, I asked him for some coke and nervously told him what just occurred.

He looked genuinely concerned and told me in his Dominican accent to, "jus' relax." His eyes said that he had also seen this same thing I was describing. It was obvious that he understood.

"Here, take dis," handing me the small bag of white powder.

He didn't ask me any questions about what I told him. I knew he wouldn't, but just telling him and getting it off of my chest made me feel much better.

After I calmed down a bit, I asked, "Can I use your bathroom to shoot this? I don't have anywhere else to go," my eyes pleading with his sense of compassion.

He looked around and out the window and said in his mixture of Spanish and English, "Si, go ahead, rapido," waving his hand toward the back of the store.

Grateful, I smiled and hurried to the back room and into a dirty little bathroom. It smelled of some chemical and obviously had never been mopped. The toilet cover was gone and stains coated the bowl. Of course, that didn't bother me; I had gotten high in many nasty places.

At the time, I considered his gesture of the use of his bathroom to be extremely nice. I think he did too. I mean, I was nothing but a homeless junkie and he knew it. He was a hard-core drug dealer. Drug dealers always look down on junkies. They think they are better than us. They don't have to sell their bodies, or live on the streets because most of them don't actually use the drugs, and the ones who do are supported by their families in the drug business. I couldn't believe he actually let me use his restroom to shoot up.

He cares.

I was completely brainwashed by the drugs I was using. Under their influence, I thought lies were the truth, and the truth was a lie. On drugs, I was completely mixed up. My mind couldn't grasp what any normal human being would have seen in this situation; only what the drugs let it see.

In the restroom, I filled the end cap of the needle with water and drew it up into the shaft. I didn't have anything to filter the coke, so I just hoped it wouldn't get clogged. Sometimes the stuff they use to cut it doesn't dissolve and can clog the needle. I poured the bag of coke, a little bigger than a packet of salt, into the end cap, squirted the water from the needle on top of it and swished it around. Then I drew it all up into the hypodermic and looked for a vein. Surprisingly, I found one almost immediately.

At last, the pain of reality was gone again and the long-awaited rush of the cocaine surged to my brain. The distinct, bitter taste of the drugs was always such a sweet welcome. I could feel my heartbeat throbbing in my head as I closed my eyes and easily forgot the unbearable events of the day.

My cycle of daily life had started again. Get high, make money, buy drugs, repeat. I was back to my old, uncaring, selfish nature; so grateful not to be dealing with the feelings that naturally would come along with the recent events. I didn't know it would still be years before I would finally face reality with courage and stop my cycle of endless bad decisions.

Chapter 2
Rape

My early childhood was filled with good things; two loving parents, my dad Jesse, or Bud as everyone calls him, my mom Judy, and an older sister named Selena. I had grandparents that were active in my life and aunts, uncles, cousins that I saw regularly. All the people a child should grow up knowing and loving were present throughout my adolescent years.

My sister and I would play with our dog, Missy, and our Siamese cat, Pyewacket, named by my mom after the cat in the movie *Bell, Book, and Candle*. When I was two, my dad found Pyewacket on the side of the road and decided he would give her to my sister and me for Christmas. He took her to the vet, had her all checked out and the vet kenneled her until Christmas Eve. We loved that cat for 18 years.

My parents also took us on family vacations every year. My favorite vacation spot was Carowinds, a theme park in North Carolina. But my favorite family trips were to an Elvis concert when I was eight years old and, in another year, our trip to Graceland. I loved Elvis. Didn't everyone? Daddy looked a little like Elvis, with black hair and blue eyes, a look I simply adored. At that time, I was a daddy's girl, and he relished the role of daddy.

We lived in a very nice neighborhood, in Wilmington, NC, in a decent sized house. It was a brick ranch with a carport that my dad eventually glassed in and made into a sunroom. I had my own decorated room and so did my sister. I had posters of my favorite actors and musicians hanging all over the walls. Life was good; there was nothing to complain about. I didn't lack or want for anything.

Our family attended a local church in the neighborhood, but we didn't go very often, just special days like Christmas, Easter, weddings or funerals, and the occasional regular Sunday morning service. We believed in the God of the Bible, but we didn't live a life of faith. We lived just like everyone else we knew, a good life with a very distant belief system.

Around age 11, I started to become a bit rebellious. I don't know of any good reason for the bad choices I started to make. Perhaps it was because I had started puberty. Perhaps, it was because I began to feel like I was different than the other kids and my sister. I felt like Selena was beautiful and I was the ugly duckling. I felt she had advantages that I didn't or couldn't possess. I was the same age as a lot of the younger siblings of my sister's friends, but we didn't get along. I just didn't fit in with that crowd. They were the popular kids. I wasn't. And, I didn't really like them anyway, because they seemed to be fake. The truth is my disdain for others stemmed from a dislike of myself.

During this time, I found myself being picked on in school by some of my classmates. My large overbite, big nose and chubby physique were the subjects of their torturous comments. Style was another issue, let's just say that it wasn't what everyone else was wearing. I hated to shop and everything my sister or mom picked out, I vetoed. The kids at school had plenty of imperfections to choose from on any given day. Their teasing really hurt my feelings, and even though my mom told me I was pretty, I knew I wasn't.

My dad tried to ease my pain. He bragged about me a lot in the younger years. In all actuality, I was good at most things I tried and that made him proud of me. He would also tell me I was pretty, but for some reason I didn't think he meant it. I am sure that was my own issue. He never made me feel ugly.

Around age 13, my Uncle Clay took me to his church with him and his wife. It was pretty cool to me as a new teenager. People were kind to me and seemed genuinely interested in who I was. The music was different than what I was used to in church, and it was a little louder as well, and I liked it. I remember the preacher asking at the end of the service if anyone wanted a relationship with Jesus Christ. I wasn't sure what he meant exactly, but I felt a tug in my heart and I responded by walking down the aisle to the altar.

After accepting Jesus into my life that day, I knew something was different inside of me, but I didn't pursue my new life in Christ any further. I didn't read my Bible like the preacher told me to, nor did I go back to church. Not realizing it then, but my decision not to follow Christ at that time would negatively effect my self-image. I would not see who I was in the eyes of God for many years to come. Also, making life altering choices and not including God or His plan for me in the process, proved to be devastating later down the road.

But for the time being, things went on as usual.

Back to the story:

I was never one to want or need a lot of friends, but I did want to be liked. The few friends I had in the neighborhood were just play friends mainly. They wouldn't understand what I was going through at school. I certainly didn't want to share my deepest feelings with them, and so they weren't any help to me and my quickly declining self-esteem.

I began to make some bad decisions that I thought would earn me respect and friendship at school. However, the choices I made only alienated me more. I realize now that those early decisions to act out were cries for help. I needed to be rescued.

I started looking for things to fill the empty hole inside, the one where my self-esteem should be. God didn't fill it because I didn't take the time to get to know Him. Despite their best efforts, my family couldn't fill it. And, the few friends I had couldn't fill it either. The rejection and loneliness were too much. I began rebelling at school to get attention; not studying, talking back to the teachers, etc. I would even pick on other kids to try and feel better about myself. Nothing worked, and I spiraled deeper into my pit, which I now know was the beginning of depression.

Back in the early 80s, it was cool to smoke. So, I started smoking. My parents smoked, my parent's friends smoked, and so did a lot of the kids at school. My mom smoked Virginia Slims, and that brand made my stomach upset, so I started stealing Salem's from my Dad. They were menthol and gave my throat a cool sensation when I inhaled.

Along with all these behavior changes, I also began to feel hopeless. Many days, I would come home from school, go into my room and cry inconsolably. My mother would ask me what was wrong, and I would just answer, "Nothing," or "I don't know." Then, I'd cry some more. Obviously, I frustrated my mom and my dad. They didn't know how to fix me or make me feel better. None of us could figure out what was missing in my life.

As a result of my pain, I began to display a drastic personality change. Would anyone notice? I didn't really want anybody to notice, especially those who loved me the most – my family. After all, what could they do about the things I was feeling, and the way I was being treated by the other kids? Even if I did talk about my feelings, I didn't want to be seen as a tattle tale, or a whiney little baby. That would just make things worse for me. So, I bottled up my pain, and all along the road to find my self-esteem, my simple rebellion turned into one bad decision after another. One of my first was also one of the worst.

***

At 14 years of age, I wondered if anyone would ever find me, the fat, ugly, big-nosed, buck-toothed girl, attractive.

My sister is so pretty, why am I so ugly? Why don't I fit in with the popular kids? What is wrong with me? The voice was very accusing. It always implied that it was me, that something was wrong with me. It also made sure that I looked at those who loved me as the bad guys.

The last 3 years of my life had been hell in school, feeling like I was abused, teased, tortured and unable to escape. One kid called me "Bucky rabbit," laughed at me incessantly, made fun of me and turned the other kids against me every day in class. I couldn't understand what I had done to him to make him so mean to me all the time. I did my best to avoid him most of the day, but we were in the same class for one hour and for that hour every single day that year, I endured his torture as he chipped away at my self-esteem. It was unbearably humiliating to have my identity, my inner self trampled on daily.

Every afternoon after school, I would jump on my 10-speed Schwinn and ride around the neighborhood just to find some relief, an escape. The ride allowed me the alone time I needed to get away from the cruel world of teenagers. Most days I would go across South College Rd., the main road in front of my neighborhood, into an apartment complex and just ride aimlessly around the parking lot. I was not allowed to cross this road, but I did anyway.

The buildings were charming and I dreamed I would one day live there. There was an in-ground pool that everyone in the complex could use, with white lounge chairs all around it. The shimmering water reflected a blue I could get lost in. I would stare into it and let the calming water relax me into oblivion. Some days, I would spend an hour or two just looking into it, daydreaming about another life. Any life but mine.

Soon, I noticed what I thought was a slightly older guy waving at me every time I came in the complex. It seemed to me to be more than just a polite hello. Although I never experienced flirting, I knew what it was. It felt good for a person of the opposite sex to actually notice me. I was always overlooked or teased by the boys I knew.

One day he stopped me and we talked for a while. I don't recall what we talked about, but I remember having butterflies in my stomach and I felt like I was on top of the world. Happy was an emotion I rarely felt, but this day I wasn't just happy, I was elated.

After seeing him for several days and chatting about whatever and anything, our relationship began to develop further. He really seemed to like me. His name was John Smith and he was 21 years old. When he told me how old he was, I felt very grown up.

Wow! This guy is interested in me!

At first, I thought he lied about his name, but later I saw it on a plaque in his living room and realized he told me the truth. I guess that gave him more credibility than my immature 14-year-old mind could comprehend. All I knew was that I found him captivating. His face wasn't much to look at, but he had a nice body and my 14-year old hormones took notice of that immediately. I became infatuated with him.

After several encounters with John outside in the parking lot, he invited me into his apartment where we watched TV and talked. Soon, I began to ride my bike to his apartment every day after school. He was always there and obviously looked forward to my arrival. The feelings I had were so overpowering. It was border-line obsession. All I could think about was John and the next time I would see him. I couldn't concentrate on anything else.

The last time I went to his house was on a Saturday. I looked forward to seeing him, and planned on spending most of the day with him. I peddled over on my bike early.

Once inside his place, I sat down and noticed he seemed different. He acted intense, not in a scary way at first, but a passionate way. We had kissed a little before, but this day he behaved poles apart from other days. He kissed me with ferocity and my heart pounded in my chest. I really didn't know what was happening.

After a few minutes of kissing on the couch, he scooped me up and took me to his bedroom where we continued kissing. I started to feel uneasy, as though I should leave. After mentioning how I felt, he lessened his intensity and assured me that everything was OK. I relaxed and felt secure in his arms once again.

I wonder if he loves me. He really seems to. He wouldn't be spending so much time with me if he didn't. Can't he just say I love you?

I longed to hear the words come from his mouth.

Just a few moments later the intensity returned with a vengeance and he was trying to take off my pants. I told him "No!", but it was no use. He had made up his mind of what he was going to do. I was so torn between the feeling of someone wanting and loving me, the ugly little fat girl, and knowing that this was wrong and that I wasn't ready. Weakly, I told him "no" again but he ignored me and completely took over.

I felt a wide range of emotions during the very short time I was there: fear, hope, anxiety, love, distress, guilt, and shame. I went limp, whimpered and repeatedly whispered, "no, no, no," until I couldn't handle it anymore and emotionally and physically checked out for the next few minutes until it was over.

The 15-minute bike ride home was the loneliest time I had spent in my entire life. I couldn't figure out how I should feel. On one hand, I thought that he must love me, because you only do that with the person you love. Then I felt violated and abused because I said no and he didn't listen.

Why couldn't he wait until I was ready? I told him no. No means no.

Then, I felt strangely happy because I thought someone might love me even though I was ugly and unpopular. I even smiled at the thought that John might really love me.

Confusion took over from that day and I had no idea what a relationship with a man should be like.

I didn't tell anyone what happened, especially my parents. They would never understand. They didn't even know who he was or that I was seeing anyone at all. I knew I would be in trouble for being over there in the first place. I rode by his apartment a few days later and he was gone, moved out, empty, with no word or explanation to me.

My heart was broken. I knew then that he didn't love me. I tried to console myself by coming up with alternative reasons for him leaving. I tried to convince myself that he got a job somewhere else and had to leave, but my heart knew the truth. I was thrown back into that role of the ugly duckling and any confidence I had been trying to claim was stripped from me along with my purity.

Should I blame myself for this? I knew I wasn't supposed to be at a man's house and if I had stayed away, it would never have happened. Yet, he still didn't have the right to rape me. I put myself in a dangerous position, one that I knew my parents wouldn't approve of and that in itself made the possibility of something bad happening even worse. And it did. I did blame myself.

The bottom line is: I lost my virginity to rape. From that point on, I was confused about relationships. I didn't know how to relate to men, and furthermore, I didn't know who I could trust. I was emotionally lost even from my own family. But because I was young, naïve, hurt, vulnerable and emotionally impaired, I had no clue what was in my best interest. My string of bad decisions had only just begun, especially when it came to men.

Chapter 3
Filling the Void

In those early teenage years, my depression and self-hatred became worse and worse. Convinced that John left because I told him no and acted like a child, I allowed the voice in my head to condemn me further into believing I was unlovable. That I was defective in some way. I knew that no one would ever love me, I felt worthless. I desperately wanted to be loved and unbeknownst to me at the time, I would do anything to try and gain that love.

As I grew older my body began to change and I wanted to show it off. I flirted incessantly with boys and wore clothes that told them I was interested and easy, even though I wasn't exactly conscious of it. Eventually, my flirtations and semi-indecent attire attracted a guy at Independence Mall. Many of the teens in our town hung out at the mall, especially during the winter. Our parents dropped us off and we roamed among the stores for hours. My childhood friend, Diane and I spent endless afternoons walking around, goofing off, smoking cigarettes and shopping.

While cruising the mall, Diane and I met a guy named Bryce. I instantly loved his name. I thought it sounded cool. I had seen him around and thought he was really good-looking, with his brown hair and gorgeous blue eyes. He had a quarterback physique. I didn't really go for jocks, but this guy was too good to be true. One day, He invited me to take a ride with him in his car and my excitement rocketed.

"Wanna go for a ride with me, just around the mall?" He asked as he flashed his perfect smile.

Knowing I wasn't allowed, I still immediately jumped in and we drove around the parking spaces. He asked me where I went to school and how old I was. I am sure I lied about my age; I never told anyone how old I really was. Every now and then he would step on the gas and make the engine roar, throwing me back into the seat. It thrilled me every time. Then, he started driving toward the stoplight onto the main road.

I protested for a minute, but then decided it wasn't a big deal. He reached over, grabbed the back of my head, pulled me over and kissed me on the mouth. Before the light changed, he unzipped his pants and shoved my head down. I squirmed and thought, if I don't do this for him, he won't like me. So, I complied and he finished before we got to the next light.

Afterwards, I pulled away and the same confusion I had experienced with John returned. Bryce took me back to the mall and dropped me off at the food court. Then he just drove away. I saw him around after that, but he never spoke to me. My heart broke again. It's hard to believe that I had such strong feelings for a guy that I had only known a few hours. Why would I fall for a guy that had done that to me? I craved attention and was attempting to get it the only way I thought I could. It was all I had to offer, the only value I had. I quickly became infatuated with men and had no idea what true love should be. I thought that if I could give a boy what he wanted, then he would like me. Never had I been more wrong.

*   *   *

 My actions and attitudes toward boys weren't the only errors in my life. I also started to test the limits in many areas. At age 14, the same year as the rape, I took my first drink. The exact time and place escape me, but the age sticks out in my mind. I can only assume it had something to do with my devastating encounter with John. Although I wouldn't drink again for quite some time, my curiosity was quenched. I wanted to know what it was like, and after I took that first drink, the drinks in a few years would come much easier. The taboo seemed to be gone. I didn't see it as a big deal anymore. Nothing bad happened, and I didn't get caught. I didn't think about its illegality. I pushed that thought to the back of my mind and went on with everyday life.

 When I began drinking regularly, I quickly found that it allowed me some breathing room in between the barrages of negative feelings I regularly experienced. Self-loathing consumed me and I began to equate my self-image with worthlessness. I was always depressed, and often wondered why I was even born. I couldn't do anything right. School was difficult and I didn't like to study. I never had to study in my younger grades, but school was different now. The work was harder and I never developed any study habits. My grades slipped drastically.

I felt like a disappointment to my parents. I didn't bring good grades home, and so they didn't smile anymore on report card day. I became lazy and didn't want to clean my room or do my chores, which further disappointed them.

I finally met some kids at school that I liked and better than that, they liked me. We called ourselves "the bleacher creatures" because we hung out by the bleachers at the football field, as far back and away from the main building and other students as we could get. We thought we were cool. There, we hung out, took little sips of whatever liquor any of us could steal from our homes, smoked cigarettes and took over-the-counter speed pills.

These kids like me for me.

We were all the same: outcasts of the social scene at school. We could relate to each other. We dressed differently than the other kids. We wore a lot of black, and absolutely shunned preppy clothes, which was the fashionable style back then. We also listened to rock music that glorified the party lifestyle: sex, drugs and rock-n-roll.

Drinking made me feel worthy, as if I belonged. I was outgoing, and fun to be around. I easily made jokes and held conversations with people. I wasn't Dana the loser. I was Dana the fun girl. At least I was with "the bleacher creatures."

When I was 16 and had been driving for a total of 6 months at best, I thought I was the best driver ever.

I'm a master. No one can drive better than me.

The next night, I put that theory to the test. I lied to my

parents and told them that I was going to a girl-friend's house and would be home by my 10pm curfew. The truth is, though, my friend and I planned to go over to my new boyfriend's house to hang out. After John and Bryce, I dated many boys. (Perhaps it was the drugs. Perhaps it was because I wanted to forget the pain of the past. But, many of their names and appearances are lost to history.) I don't remember much about this particular boyfriend except that he was 18 or 19 and living on his own.

I had finally begun to grow out of my awkwardness, filling out and becoming prettier. I used my newfound looks to attract men. I was still looking for someone to love me. Most of the time, the attraction was purely physical. I assumed that they would immediately like me once they got to know me and then they would possibly fall in love, but that never happened.

When we got to my boyfriend's house, we saw that he and his friend had bought some vodka and orange-juice and set out four small glasses. The small rented house was dark and stank like cigarettes. There wasn't much furniture, just an old couch and a table straight from the 50s. It had metal legs and a Formica top with four chairs that didn't match. A TV and stereo were in the corner set up on a couple of milk crates. A few cassette tapes lay scattered on the floor. I thought it looked cool. In reality, it was quite ugly, but it was theirs and no grownups were there to ruin the fun.

We started playing a drinking game called Quarters, where you bounce a quarter on the table and try to make it land in a glass of beer or in this case Vodka and orange juice. If you bounced the quarter into the glass, you got to pick the person you wanted to drink the concoction. I had played the game before, but not to the extent that we did that night. Anyway, I lost severely.

I became so drunk that I didn't realize how late it was. My curfew had long passed. Finally, after noticing the hour, I stumbled outside to my car, and blacked out. I don't know how I was able to drive home. That part of the night is still a complete mystery to me. But I know I did the driving. I didn't have any help. Thinking back now, I don't even remember what happened to my friend. I do, however, remember arriving home, climbing out of my car and seeing the fuzzy shadow of a giant in the doorway of my parent's house. Taking several steps backwards, and then propelling myself forward, I arrested myself about 4 feet from the giant who had mysteriously transformed himself into my father. Then, I fell face first at his feet over the threshold.

Minutes later, I was in the bathroom throwing up until I had nothing left to come out, which was followed by a string of dry heaves. My body made sure that every bit of poison inside of me was gone. Thankfully my body was much smarter than I was.

Meanwhile, my parents waited for me in my bedroom. I don't know what was worse: throwing up in the bathroom, or dreading the wrath that faced me in the other room. As my mind raced with the thoughts of my sentence, my body wracked with wretches. I decided I did not care about the consequences. What was the worst thing that could happen to me? They weren't gonna kill me. And even if they did, so what?

They grounded me. I couldn't go out, I couldn't use the phone. All I could do was go to school and come straight home. But, it didn't matter to me. It wouldn't be forever, just a couple of weeks or so, and then back to normal. This wasn't going to stop me. I finally had friends and people in my life who wanted to be with me. I was finally having fun. The void was being filled, or so I thought.

I entered a new phase in my life and had no concept of how dangerous it was. I was cool, a rule-breaker. I and I alone made the rules and decisions in my life. That night, I could have killed someone or myself. Rebellious and uncaring, my spiral downward had only just begun.

Chapter Four
It Should Have Been the Most Difficult Decision of My Life

By the time I turned 18 years old, the age of legal adulthood, my resolve not to care about anything continued and my partying grew to new levels. The escalation of substance abuse among youth had been predicted by teachers in drug awareness classes throughout the years. It starts with cigarettes and alcohol and progresses to pot, then to pills and acid. At the time, I thought their forecast was ridiculous. It might happen to some people, but not to me. I was in control of my life and I controlled my actions. Nevertheless, I evolved just as predicted.

I was smoking pot on a regular basis, it was like the very air I breathed. Drinking started around seven or eight o'clock in the evening and didn't stop until the bar was closed. My fake ID looked absolutely nothing like me; however, it worked like a charm. I also took prescription pills several times a week and when I took them it was never just one. I never did anything in moderation. I took several at a time and several different kinds at a time.

My then boyfriend, James, was also like air for me. I didn't recognize it then, but I had a desperate need to have someone in my life whom I believed loved me for me. I would do anything for that one person to gain the love I felt I needed from them. As stupid as it sounds, he made me feel lovable, even when he was being a jerk, which was more often than not. For a long time, I felt that no one would ever love me, especially after John raped me and Bryce took advantage of my obvious self-esteem issues.

Another pattern I hadn't noticed then, but see clearly now, was that I became infatuated with men who showed me attention. I'd obsess over them utterly and completely. In my mind, I convinced myself that if I acted a certain way or did certain things, they would feel the same way about me.

Making James love me was my goal, my focus, my need. I wouldn't do anything without considering what reaction he would have as a result.

James and I first met one night when my best friend Sue and I were on the way to a party. We stopped for gas and there he was, walking down the street. He started talking to us and after he explained that his car was broken down, I invited him to the party. He accepted. I found him very attractive. He was tall and thin, with straight light brown hair to his shoulders and it was slightly feathered on the sides. I thought he resembled a musician and I loved the whole rock-n-roll, bad boy image.

Once at the party, we drank and talked. He was much more social than I was. I hung back with Sue and some other people I knew, but he mingled with everyone. Every now and then, he would come over and talk to me and flirt. Every time he did, the butterflies in my stomach would make themselves known. Soon, he only talked with me and we sat on a sofa, drank beer and laughed for the rest of the night.

James and I became inseparable after that night. I spent the majority of my time driving him places. I felt useful helping him get to work or to the store. He was a struggling singer and I loved the fact that he needed me. Every day after school, I picked him up and we would smoke a joint and go run his errands.

We were also having unprotected sex. I mentioned once that we should be using protection, but he didn't want to. He said it made him feel closer to me and I loved that. Plus, I didn't want to argue with him for fear he would find someone else who wouldn't fuss about using protection. So, I just stopped being concerned about it.

After James and I were together for about six months, I missed my period. After telling him I needed to get a pregnancy test, he seemed extremely aggravated with me. However, he finally agreed to go with me to the store. Once we got back to his apartment, I went in the bathroom and took the test. My mind raced with the possibilities and then the obvious fears of him not being happy about it if it was positive. Anxiously, I waited for the lines to appear.

Deep down, I wanted him to be excited about the chance of being a father, that our love for each other may have created another life. Maybe he would feel the same way as I did about it, that it would be me, him and our baby against the world. I created a world within my mind that didn't exist. James didn't love me. He was using me, but I would never admit that to myself. I kept hoping.

Yes, two lines! My initial reaction in the bathroom was full of excitement. But, I tried not to show too much enthusiasm when I told him it was positive. I had to weigh his reaction. I thought it might take him a little while to get used to the idea.

"Make an appointment to get an abortion," he said coldly, "I'll find the money to pay for it."

He walked out of the apartment and left me standing there all alone. I was crushed. *Why doesn't he want to have a baby with me? Why doesn't he love me or at least this baby inside of me? It's part of him, too.* Immediately, those unwelcome and always nearby feelings of worthlessness and inadequacy came flooding into my head.

It should have been the most difficult decision of my life, but it was made in just a few seconds and not even by me. I knew from his reaction, that if I didn't get the abortion, he would leave me. I thought I couldn't live without him. I thought that my life meant nothing without him.

In an effort to comfort myself, I recalled all of the news and scientific reports on fetuses. *This thing inside of me isn't even a real baby yet.* I rationalized it away and with tears in my eyes, I made the appointment.

About two weeks later James and I went to the clinic in Wilmington. I was scared and unsure of what I really wanted to do. I loved the baby inside me, but it was not tangible. It couldn't fill the void that I would have without James, at least not yet. I chose to stay with what I already had, even if it was a far inferior option. It didn't matter that it wasn't a good relationship. It was still a relationship.

Something was better than nothing.

The clinic was like any other doctor's office: a waiting room with fabric and leather chairs, a few small printed sofas and end tables with magazines fanned out on them. The wallpaper was like you would find in any workplace: nondescript with abstract swirls and flecks. The receptionist's area was behind sliding glass, just to the left as you walked in through the tinted glass front door. The waiting room to the right held about nine or 10 people, all women, some mothers, some daughters, some that could be just friends, but no men, except James. It was very quiet and tense. No one said a word in the waiting room. They just stared down at the floor, obviously trying to be invisible.

I wonder why, if abortion is ok and the fetus is not really a baby that people try to hide the fact that they are having an abortion. If it's just tissue, why is it shameful? Everyone recognizes the seriousness and permanency of abortion, even if not everyone agrees that it is wrong, but society helps us ease any guilt we may feel by saying that it is a "choice."

"Dana McLawhon." They called me from doors that led to the back. I tried not to connect with those words. It was my name, but I didn't want it to be so personal. Maybe I could separate myself somehow from what I was doing. Nervously, I got up, walked over to the voice and we disappeared behind the door.

"Have a seat here, and someone will be right with you," the nurse said as she stood outside an office and pointed to a chair inside, while placing my paperwork in a bin outside the door. Her rhythmic motions told me she did this all the time. The thought actually made me feel more comfortable, knowing there were many girls who made the decision to abort their child.

After a minute or two, a lady came in and we met for about five minutes. She asked me a few questions. "How old are you? Is anyone forcing you to do this? Are you sure this is what you wish to do?" That seemed to be the extent of her concern. Of course, all of my answers were lies with the exception of my age.

She walked me back to an examination room with a small changing area and told me to put on a gown and when I was done, I was to come out and have a seat on the table.

The Doctor came in and said, "Ms. McLawhon?" At that point, I hated that name and didn't want to hear it again. The rest is a blank to me. It amazes me how the mind can just block out some traumatic experiences and allow others to remain. It must be some sort of survival technique.

Once it was done, James was back to his old self. We continued like nothing had ever happened. I happily took him everywhere and he happily used me to do so. I put the abortion out of my mind and justified it by telling myself that James wanted it and he loved me because I did it. I proved I loved him by going through with what he wanted, no matter how much I didn't want to do it.

We continued to have unprotected sex and only a year later, I was pregnant again. I was convinced we could make a life together now. After all, we had been together for a year and a half and we loved each other.

James had the very same reaction as the first time. I was devastated. Again, the dream world I made up in my mind had crumbled. Again, I was afraid that if I kept the baby, I would lose James and he was more important to me than life itself.

I made the appointment and he didn't even go with me to the clinic. I talked one of my friends into taking me. I slipped deeper into self-loathing and wasn't sure exactly why. I knew that I didn't want to have an abortion, but everyone said it was alright, it wasn't a baby, it was just a circumstance that could be changed, legally. But inside, I was falling apart.

My decision to have another abortion was based on nothing but James' demand and my lack of self-esteem and neediness. I had absolutely no counsel from anyone. The clinic didn't discuss any alternatives and the world said it was perfectly alright. All I had to depend on for support was James and the cold clinic.

My relationship with my parents had been deteriorating for several years, so I wasn't going to go to them and admit that I needed them. James didn't want a baby, and he didn't have to have one sucked out of him. He had nothing to lose. The clinic just took the money and my babies without ever offering another option. If I knew then what I know now, I would have given them the money just to give me an alternative solution to my problem.

I justified the abortions by telling myself that it was legal, so it can't be a big deal. I just got the abortions, and continued to numb my feelings with pot, alcohol, and pills and went on with life. I tried to see it as no big deal and decided I didn't care anyway. It was so much easier not to care. I may have killed myself had I cared.

Chapter Five
Add Money to the Equation

Up to this point in my short nineteen and a half years, I hadn't made many good choices for my life at all. There were, however, two good things I was able to manage thus far. One was to graduate from high school; the other was to go on to college or in my case technical school.

I enrolled at Cape Fear Tech and was studying to be a Paralegal. I didn't want to be a paralegal. As a matter of fact, I had no idea what I wanted to be. Honestly, I didn't really know everything that was available to me, and the things I did know about didn't appeal to me at all. I never met with a guidance counselor to discuss occupations. Funny, but I still don't know what I want to become when I grow up.

So, I was nineteen and a half, going to technical college, drinking as much as possible, smoking pot and taking pills, still dating James who was not in love with me and I was still very much un-in-love with myself. Through those years, I worked at Winn Dixie as a cashier; Crusty's Pizza as a pizza maker and order taker; and several other odd jobs. My favorite job was at the pizza joint on Market Street in Wilmington.

I liked it because the tips were good and I had had grown out of that awkward, ugly stage, and I knew how to gain the attention from the male customers. I thrived on the flirty little comments, and gestures. While at work, my self-esteem seemed high, but as soon as I was back with James, I once again became that ugly girl who was desperate for his attention. This should have proven that my self-esteem didn't come from my appearance or from other people.

Every day, during lunch time at school and also between the end of the school day and starting work, I went to James' apartment to see him. The apartment was one bedroom, one bath and a kitchen above the detached garage of an old lady whom I never saw. The rooms were in desperate need of paint which was considered typical of the dwellings of house painters. It seems he could have found time to paint, being that he rarely worked at his painting job. The walls were badly stained with nicotine and the bathtub and toilet looked as if at any minute, they could go crashing to the lower level due to the rotten flooring in the bathroom. There were no window treatments, just old gray metal mini-blinds that may have once been white. There were no closets or storage areas, so everything in need of storing, was placed in the corner of the kitchen where a small dinette would have fit nicely. The bedroom held an old scratched up chest of drawers and a set of bunk beds on the top of which slept our friend Ronnie.

Ronnie was a good friend to me, at least better than any of the others. When James wasn't around, he would always tell me that I could do better than James and that he didn't treat me right. I knew Ronnie was telling the truth, but I could never convince myself he was right. At least, I could never convince the part of me that believed I could make James love me. I talked to Ronnie about everything, but he was James' friend first and loyalty wouldn't allow him to say anything to James about my treatment.

* * *

One day, after my lunch break from school, I left James' apartment and was going back to school. I was traveling at 45 miles per hour and all of a sudden everything was black. When I woke there was a man standing outside my car window.

"Just be still, you are going to be OK," he said in a very calming voice.

I was very confused and then I noticed the front end of my beloved, red, 1975 Datsun 280Z was inches away from my lap. The beautiful gift my parents gave me was crumpled and broken. That car was my pride and joy. It was the only thing that I owned that made me feel cool.

Feeling extremely fuzzy, I asked, "What happened?"

"You were in an accident. Someone hit you head on," said the very concerned man in a soothing tone.

"Who hit me?"

"He did," pointing to a man standing in the middle of the road talking to another gentleman beside a pick-up truck.

The man who was helping me protested, but I pulled myself out of the car anyway. I held on to the top of the bent door, pointed at the man who had hit me, and proceeded to verbally thrash him. "Look what you did to my car, you idiot! Look what you did to my car! You idiot! You idiot!"

The man, who had been tending to me, convinced me to sit back down and relax. I looked up into the mirror hanging loosely from the broken windshield and saw the deep red color of my car staring back at me and then I realized it was my face covered in blood. My teeth were broken and twisted in my mouth. Some were missing.

"Finally, the ambulance," said my new caretaker, obviously relieved.

The EMTs gathered some of my teeth from the floorboard of my pitiful car and took me to the emergency room where I was evaluated. There were no internal injuries, but major oral damage. They told my parents to take me immediately to an oral surgeon. When I got there, I was given some of the best drugs I had taken to date and my two front teeth and one lower tooth were re-inserted. The others couldn't be found.

Months went by without school or work. I was too embarrassed to go out with my new snaggletooth look. I wouldn't smile, even at James or my family. My self-esteem issues were more damaged than ever.

I was going to doctors quite often, orthopedic for my knees, which were jammed into the console of the car, and a chiropractor for my back, which did absolutely no good. I also saw my oral surgeon, who decided that my teeth were not going to stay put and so prescribed my need for a bridge. Thankfully, they were able to obtain the molds from my days when I wore braces, which were just about a year before the wreck. They made a permanent bridge, which looks just like my real teeth before the accident.

Meanwhile, my parents contacted a lawyer and found out the man who hit me was a career criminal. He created accidents to collect the insurance money and the day he hit me, he was trying to create an accident with the man driving in front of me. My lawyer also found out that he had very minimal insurance. It was nowhere near enough to pay my medical bills.

Thankfully, our health insurance paid for my medical bills and the underinsured motorist coverage that my parents had on my car paid out $42,000 for injuries suffered. It didn't come all at once though. I would receive 3 payments over the next nine years. I acquired my first check in the amount of $22,000 not long after we settled in court.

Once I had the money, James became much more attentive. He definitely needed me now. I paid for everything, going out, partying, pot, and food. I even paid his rent on a few occasions. I was no longer the desperate little girl needing to be loved. I was now the puppeteer with my puppet or dummy, as it was, and this lifestyle felt so much better than before. It didn't bother me that I knew he didn't love me. I was now in control. He did what I wanted him to do, just like I did what he wanted to do when I got the abortions.

I dropped out of school because, stupidly, I thought I could live forever on $22,000. I bought an old mobile home and perched it in the Circle R Mobile Home Estates. I was big time! I was a home owner. I had two bedrooms, an eat-in kitchen, a dining room with a bay window and a bathroom.

The money ran low quickly, so James taught me how to paint the interiors of houses so I could get a job. I met with his supervisor and lied, telling him that I painted houses for my Dad in Raleigh for five years and had plenty of experience. I started the next day.

By this time, I was 20 years old and headed for a life of hard labor and non-existent love. I made sure that James knew that every three years I would be getting another check over nine years' time. I hoped that this information would keep him hanging on.

The partying continued, and on my twenty-first birthday, James turned me on to cocaine for the first time. I loved it, but it was very expensive. It wouldn't be added to my regular portfolio of drugs until a few years later.

Not long after that, James became tired of me. I was out of money and it would be another year or so before anymore would come. We broke up and I was devastated. I remember the day it happened. I still had the phone in my hand and I crumpled to the floor in agony. Sounds came out of me that I didn't know existed. Wailing and crying mixed with spurts of anger and hate flowed out. I thought I would rather be dead than to live without him. I'd rather he be dead than to see him with someone else. The drugs and alcohol increased after that and successfully drowned out my depression for a time. I didn't realize then how far down the road of destruction I actually was.

I quickly grew weary of painting houses. I was lazy and it was too much work for me. There had to be a way to make quick money and not have to work for it. I was buying my pot from a guy named Sammy about five miles out of town. I talked to him and he said I could sell for him. He taught me how to bag, weigh, and sell pot. Customers came quickly. People I knew told their friends and they told their friends and so on and so on. I became a master at weighing out bags of pot by feel and always gave a little extra to keep my customers happy.

Everyone who came over to buy pot from me was required to stay for at least 15 or 20 minutes so that it didn't look as if I had a revolving-door pharmacy at my place. I always offered free bong hits for their time.

All of a sudden, I had "friends" coming out of the woodwork. In my distorted view, I thought people liked me. In reality, I just had something they wanted. There was no loyalty there, if someone else had better weed, I would have no friends.

I made it my business for that never to happen. I kept the best all the time.

Chapter 6

My First Arrest

I had an abundance of so-called friends. I sold good pot, at a great price and I was fun to be around.

On the nights that it was open, I hung out at the Mad Monk, a local club. Everyone I knew hung out there; it was the only rock-n-roll bar in town. It had two levels; the upstairs looked out over the mosh-pit in front of the stage. Someone would always stumble out of the pit bleeding or injured in some way or another. Peg, I will introduce you to her in a few, and I went in the pit occasionally, if we were drunk enough. It seemed as if the slamming around got a little friendlier when we went in. Neither of us ever got hurt.

On either side of the stage were two huge speakers. I spent a lot of the night in front of them, rocking out as the bands played. It's a wonder I can hear anything at all these days. The music was so loud that you couldn't hear the person right next to you.

Everything was made out of rustic wood and it was always very dark inside. There were two bars, one upstairs and one downstairs. The place always stunk like stale cigarettes and beer. It doesn't sound so appealing now, but then it was my favorite place to be. It felt good to finally be around people who liked me and I liked as well. I felt a lot better about myself on the surface level, but inside there was still a huge, empty hole. I did my best to fill it every night with Rum and Coke, Natural Light, pot and pills.

Drinking and partying with the customers and bands that passed through were my favorite pastimes. The bartenders all knew me and always comp'd me several beers per night in return for delivering their weed to the bar. I felt like a V.I.P. every time I was there.

One day, while I was in my trailer bagging pot, there was a knock at the door. I pushed the tray I used to hold my paraphernalia under the couch and went to the peephole. It was my good friend Johnny who played lead guitar for a local band called The Peak and some girl with long wavy dirty-blonde hair.

Opening the door, I immediately asked, "Who's that?" pointing at her.

"This is Peg. She's cool. Known her forever," Johnny responded.

"Okay," I said, "Come on in," granting entry. I looked outside for unfamiliar cars or people after they crossed the threshold. I noticed that they were riding in a gold Porsche. I remember thinking, *cool car, she must have money.*

We sat down and Johnny introduced us. "Dana, this is Peg. She goes to school in New York, but she is from here. She wants to buy some weed. Cool?"

Still a bit skeptical, but trusting that Johnny wouldn't bring someone to me he didn't know, I asked, "How much do you want?"

"Can I get a half ounce?" she said, digging in her bag for the money.

Peg was kind of short, not a beauty queen by most people's standards, but very cute. She reeked of money. Her outfit of jeans and a shirt were tied together with very trendy accessories. Her wallet made of black and white horsehair, her Harley Davidson motorcycle boots and jacket, her belt with the big buckle all said rock-and-roll. Her jewelry also reeked of money, not a matching set, but very put together with turquoise and red coral, all flowed into a great package. I was always skeptical of new people, but I felt very at ease with Peg for some reason.

Reaching down under the couch to pull out my stash, I asked her where she went to school in New York.

"Sarah Lawrence College. I'm taking acting classes and stuff. It's cool."

I handed her two tightly rolled up sandwich baggies of fluffy green buds with little red hairs on them. It was the best stuff I'd gotten in a while.

She shook one open, smelled it and asked, "You wanna smoke?"

"Nope, it's on me," I said, "I don't sell it to ya and then go and smoke yours all up."

Johnny began explaining my rules about coming to the house while I grabbed my guitar-shaped bong from beside the couch, loaded it up and passed it to her first.

When I saw that she really inhaled, I relaxed. It was common knowledge that an undercover cop wouldn't inhale. So, I always took care to watch, even though it was too late. It still relaxed my mind to know that no one was going to barge through the front door and arrest me at any minute.

We smoked and talked for a while. By the time they left, we had all made plans to meet at the Mad Monk that night and hang out. Johnny's band, The Peak, was playing and Peg and I could hang out together and drink. I liked her. She seemed like a nice person and any friend of Johnny's was a friend of mine.

Peg and I hit it off from the start; we became best friends and pretty much inseparable. I knew that she wasn't using me for drugs because she always bought plenty and she shared hers with me. I found out later that she was from one of the wealthier families in Wilmington and that made me comfortable that she wasn't after something she could get from me. Now Johnny, on the other hand, was a poor guitarist and we all knew he was out to get a free high and free drinks, but it was cool because he was a musician and that was just what they did.

Several months went by selling pot and hanging out until all hours of the night. I thought I was so smart, that I couldn't get busted. And I didn't get busted, at least not in my trailer for selling pot.

A friend of mine picked me up one night to go hang out down at Carolina Beach. There was really nothing to do there except go to some of the bars. So, after smoking a joint on the way, we stopped at McDonalds to get something to take care of the munchies. As we pulled out of the parking lot, he steered directly in front of a police car.

Immediately the blue lights came on. Being a dealer, I was already nervous and a bit paranoid, especially since we were high.

We sat in the truck until the officer said, "Step out of the vehicle."

We complied. As soon as I got to the back of the truck, I realized I had left my purse on the front seat. I thought, *crap, maybe he won't look in it.*

No such luck. He walked to the back of the truck and said, "Who is Dana McLawhon?"

"I am," in a defeated whisper.

"Please put your hands on the truck and spread your legs."

Again, I complied, thankful I didn't have anything else on me. I didn't think they would arrest me for the little bit of pot I had in my bag. It was so little they probably would just scare me and let me go.

Again, no such luck. He started reading me my rights. I don't know where my friend was by this time. I was so consumed with what was happening to me. I was getting arrested for a roach. Not even a half a joint. Unbelievable I thought. *Don't they have anything better to do with their time? Aren't there murderers out there they needed to be concerned with? I am just a person smoking a little pot. I am not hurting anyone.*

Although, at that moment, I was just a person smoking a little pot, the rest of the time I was definitely hurting someone. I was hurting myself and all my customers. I justified it by telling myself that they would get it from somewhere else, if I wasn't selling it to them. I was officially the justification queen. I could justify anything and make it seem, at least to myself, that I was not doing anything wrong.

I had allowed two extremely dangerous things to enter my life. One was not caring. I didn't care about anything. But if I found myself caring about something, then I was good at justifying it away. That was my second danger.

I was arrested that night on charges of simple possession. I called one of my customers to come and get me out of jail. I hadn't had much contact with my parents outside of Thanksgiving and Christmas, so there was no way I would call them; especially since I would have received another lecture.

Of course, when I went to court, I pled not guilty, knowing full well I was guilty. I took no responsibility for anything in my life; I just excused it away or completely denied it. It was such a relief when I was sentenced to time served. I went home to my trailer and smoked enough bong hits to put me in a coma for a few hours.

After that incident, I became much more careful about the people who came to the trailer. It wasn't long before I started noticing a strange car parked down the street a bit. It was always parked in the curve, nearly out of view, but I could just see the two men sitting in the front seat from my kitchen window.

I was being watched.

Chapter 7
No Regrets-Big Apple Bound

I devised a new method of distribution to take care of my problem of being watched by the police at my home. I would deliver the marijuana to my customers. I completely shut down my in-home drug depot and began my own personal distribution service. The minimum delivery amount would be one half of an ounce. That should make enough money for me to justify the gas and time spent delivering.

They can't stop me; I am too smart for them.

One day the phone rang, "Dana, it's your mom."

"Hey."

"Can you come over here? Your father and I need to talk to you."

Hesitantly I answered, "Sure."

I knew that whatever it was they wanted couldn't be good, so I took my time in getting over there. They only lived fifteen minutes away, but a few hours later I pulled up in the driveway and went inside. Both of my parents were home. I acted like I had everything in control when I saw them, but their faces were more serious than usual this time and I became concerned. Sitting down on the rust colored corduroy sofa, I braced myself for what they had to say.

"Dana, the police were here today."

It felt as though someone had sucked the air out of my lungs. Trying to appear nonchalant I shrugged a wimpy, "Why?"

"They said you are involved with a drug dealer in Whiteville. And that they have seen your car at his home many times in the last few months. What's going on?"

"I don't know any drug dealer in Whiteville," I lied, "who is it?" Fishing for information and fingering the ridges in the rust colored, corduroy couch. Lying no longer seemed wrong to me. The lies came out like truth. My parents knew my word couldn't be trusted and I knew they didn't believe me. Still, I didn't care,

I was hopeful that they would reply with the name of a person I didn't really know and that the issue at hand would just go away. I hoped that somehow, they were misinformed and the police had made a mistake.

"Sammy Marshall," she said, confirming what I already knew. My heart sank deep into my stomach.

Acting as if they were stupid, but scared out of my wits, I insisted, "Sammy isn't a drug dealer. He's just a guy," hoping my lie would convince people otherwise, who already knew the real truth.

"Dana, we are concerned about you. The police told us that they are watching you and it is only a matter of time before they come and get you. You need to stop what you're doing." The look on my mom's face was of obvious concern, but I was so lost in my lies that I couldn't turn back now.

"I am not doing anything!" I yelled. I was mad at the people who loved me because I couldn't face the reality of my life. I needed to be mad at them, to justify the lies I was telling them.

I kept waiting for the doorbell to ring and the police to come in and arrest me. I thought my parents had set me up. But, they didn't.

After the confrontation from my parents was over, I left in the car I bought from my parents a few months before. It was a dark green, two-door, 1982 Cutlass Supreme. The ceiling liner was falling down and I had tacked it up with pins. I didn't take good care of it at all. As a matter of fact, about two months later, I blew the motor in it.

While riding back to my trailer, I pondered my options while I watched in the rear-view mirror for the police.

I was overwhelmed by recent events in my life at that point. I had been numbing my feelings of self-loathing with alcohol and drugs, but paranoia, a brand-new feeling, was just too much. Extreme depression ensued. No amount of drugs could take away the paranoia. I found myself constantly looking out the window and I was skeptical of everyone I saw. I knew that the police were watching me and I convinced myself that it was just a matter of minutes or seconds before they would come smashing through my door. My only outlet was writing. This poem was written on April 15, 1991, as I entered a new darker era in my life:

> I am still so young, so much time left
> But maybe not, no one knows when time will stop

> I have no control over my thoughts, my decisions
> I want to know who does
> Who is this person, thing, that has control over me?
> Is it Satan? Am I in hell? Help me!

I wrote the following on the same day:

> Lying here waiting for my time to come
> I see things so close, but so out of reach
> I see myself going for them
> But I always trip and fall
> It is best now, that I have forced my death
> No more worry or problems that filled my mind
> I don't want to wait for the end of time
> Please forgive me for the things I've done
> And commend me for others
> I wasn't all bad, I wasn't evil
> In my eyes.

I hadn't done or taken anything to kill myself, but I wanted to. I didn't try because I was afraid of what was on the other side for me. I was a coward on all sides.

* * *

Peg and I were hanging out all the time now since she took a semester off from college. Jumping in her Porsche and traveling to live music shows all over North Carolina, Virginia and West Virginia. We closed every bar we went to, no matter how late it stayed open. There were many times when we got invited to stay after hours and party with the band.

On one of these nights, I met Thomas, a guitar tech from a band called Wrathchild America. We hit it off right away. He lived in New Jersey so we talked mostly on the phone and I would go see him in different cities along the eastern seaboard with Peg.

Thomas was a sweet guy. He treated me like I was special and with respect. He always asked me if I needed anything, he opened doors for me, bought me drinks and small gifts. If anyone bothered me at the bar, he set them straight. I felt as if he protected me. He wasn't a big guy by any means, but he was feisty. His dark brown hair was always messy and his brown eyes were peaceful.

We had been seeing each other for about six months when I told him about the situation with police coming to my parent's house. He immediately asked me to move to New Jersey and live with him. I kind of laughed it off, even though the thought of him wanting to protect me made me feel good. I had only been to New York once with Peg. I really loved it up there, but I didn't have enough money to move.

Soon it became obvious to me that I needed to move out of my trailer. The car on the curve was stationed there around the clock and I knew it wouldn't be long before I was on my way to jail. I had to quit selling pot and get a real job. So, I applied and got a job at

Speedy Oil Change and Tune Up as the receptionist.

I asked my parents if I could move back in with them and they said yes. I am sure they thought that I was trying to turn my life around, but I was really just looking for a way to party more and not get into any trouble. So, I quit selling pot, went to work regularly and partied even more.

* * *

"Yes! Four thousand dollars!" I had finally received the next installment from my insurance settlement. Immediately, I called Thomas.

"Now you can move up here and we can be together," he said.

"I know, I can hardly wait. I'm gonna go and tell my parents and start packing right now!" It was January 1991. I was 22 years old.

My parents were not surprised. I think there was nothing I could do at this point to shock them. I know their initial thought was that I wouldn't make it up there and that I would be home soon. However, I was determined to make it. In the back of my mind, a sense of accomplishment began to form. If I can make it in New York, I will have some self-worth. I wanted to prove it to myself, to any and everyone else who thought I was a failure. I desperately wanted to be more than I was turning out to be. This move, I hoped, would give me the change I was looking for.

About a week or so later, I packed up my new to me, gently used, Nissan Sentra and began my journey. I remember thinking: *I don't want any regrets. I don't ever want to say, "I wish I moved to New York when I had the chance. I wonder what could have been."*

Chapter Eight
Building My Castle

The nine-hour drive felt liberating. I was fleeing my former life, my former self, and soon I would be in Jersey City, New Jersey. A new state, a new town, a new life, a new person…or so I thought. I hadn't fully digested the saying; "wherever you go, there you are." There was no way I was going to get away from me.

By the time I reached New Jersey, the snowfall was incredible. I just knew it was a huge nor'easter. Compared to what we see in Wilmington, NC it was a full-fledged blizzard. My little car struggled to stay on a straight path, much like me in life. So, I kept on moving and slowly crept toward my destination.

Finally, I reached Thomas's neighborhood and shockingly found a parking spot not too far from the house. The house was divided into two separate apartments upstairs and a basement apartment downstairs plus storage area. The upper levels shared an entrance door and foyer. The steps that lead to the glass entry door were cement with brick sides. Once inside, it was scantily decorated with a small table and a runner that showed the way to the first apartment door. The basement entry was outside, down an encasement of dirty, gray, concrete stairs, overrun with dead weeds and vines. Of course, this was where my new home would be located. At the time, I didn't notice how ugly it really was. The thought of living so close to New York, on my own, was tremendous.

I had about $3500 left in my pocket and two pounds of weed. Thomas told me weed was more expensive in New Jersey and maybe I should bring some up. So, I did. I still had no concept of the value of a dollar. I thought that my money would last quite a while. In reality, after about a month, I realized the inevitable…I needed a job.

So, Thomas brought home a newspaper and I started over the classifieds for jobs in the city. I answered a few ads including one for a secretarial position on 37th Street in Manhattan. The details escape me now of the application process, but it wasn't long before I received a call to come in for an interview. The day before the interview, Thomas asked me how I was going to get there.

"Drive," I said.

"You can't drive to the city during the day."

Defiantly, as usual, "Why not?"

"You will never find a parking spot and it costs a lot to park in a garage - if there is even one close by, not to mention the traffic," he said, as if I was stupid.

"Fine, how am I gonna get there?"

"The PATH to the subway. I'll take you to the PATH train in the morning and get you a subway map. It's easy," he said, sounding like more of a help now than a smarty pants. "It will take you about an hour to get there."

"An hour? You gotta be kidding me!"

I was used to about a 10-minute commute at the most back home. I decided that I had no choice and I would just suffer through it.

About a week later, the phone rang and Thomas yelled for me. We lived in a two-room apartment. I never understood why he always yelled. I picked up the phone and Brenda, the office manager, told me that I got the job.

I was now the secretary for Bob Paganucci Design, Inc., a prominent graphic design firm. What an awesome feeling. I was making it on my own in New York City! But, I was nervous that my new employers would find out that I didn't have as much experience as I lead them to believe. I was good at faking everything. I faked being a house painter and now I was going to fake being a secretary. The worst thing that could happen is I wouldn't be able to pull it off. I wasn't too worried though, I still had that ability not to care, so if it didn't work out, I would just find something else to do.

It turned out that I was good at faking the actual work as well. I performed well at my new job and got along wonderfully with the designers as well as the boss. It was like a little family. Thinking back, most of us were misfits. That is probably why I fit in so well.

Brenda was around 50 and never married, no kids, and lived in Connecticut by herself. My favorite designer was Ralph. He was gay. Ralph and I hung out sometimes at the bar around the corner from the office. He was a lot of fun. Rob, the techie, was just strange. It is almost impossible to describe why or how he was a misfit, but if you met him you would immediately figure out that he was one. Mr. Paganucci and his son Frank were not misfits. They were very normal, businessmen.

Not long after I started working, Thomas and I broke up. There was no real reason other than we were not compatible as a couple. We remained friends and he let me stay with him until I could move out on my own. It wasn't long before I began the hunt for an affordable apartment.

Living in Manhattan was not an option, it was so expensive and if I wanted something decent, I would have to live in one of the other boroughs. I began by looking at ads in the newspaper. I saw one for a room in an apartment shared by two other girls. I answered the ad and went to Park Slope, Brooklyn to view the apartment and meet my potential roomies.

Park Slope is one of the nicer areas of Brooklyn and the brownstone was so cute from the outside. It was a four-story walkup and in my excitement, I felt like I floated up the stairs with no effort at all. At $300 per month, I could afford it with no problem.

The girls and I hit it off immediately and a couple of weeks later, my parents drove up with my stuff and I moved in. My parents weren't happy at first about my move to New York, but when they saw me and how happy I seemed and where I would be staying, they accepted it a little better. I got the feeling that they were proud of me again. It was a feeling that I hadn't experienced in quite some time. Honestly, I hadn't given them any reason to be proud of me in quite some time. Maybe it was just me, but I thought they were proud that I made a move on my own and was making it work; a fresh start for my life. Little did I know, I would be making several fresh starts over the next 10-years.

* * *

Peg was back at college and we saw each other quite often. We hung out in the East Village every weekend and on several days during the week. Our favorite spot was a little smoky, hole-in-the-wall, bar on St. Mark's Place called Finian's Rainbow. We got to know the bartenders and the clientele well. We became regulars and were the life of the party. Drinking and smoking pot out back in the courtyard, with whomever had good stuff, was practiced often. I maintained my job and Peg maintained her schoolwork. I was functioning with a hangover most days, but I was paying my bills, so I didn't see anything wrong with my lifestyle.

This continued for several months until my roommates questioned the funny smell coming out of my room. I had begun to smoke pot up there and they didn't like it. They asked me to move out, but kindly, they gave me time to find a place.

I had met a girl through Peg who was looking for a roommate. Her name escapes me now, but we had partied a few times and got along wonderfully. We found a one-bedroom on Houston and Mott St. in Manhattan. I was moving to Manhattan! It was a brand-new building and we were ecstatic. Right down the street from Chinatown and around the corner from Little Italy, we had hit it big. Everything I could possibly want was just a short walk or cab ride away. Who could ask for anything better than this? I was on cloud nine and invincible. No one could knock me down, not even me.

About a year later, my roommate decided to move back to her hometown. I had recently gotten a raise at work and was able to afford substantially more in rent per month. I began, once again, the hunt for a living space. I had become accustomed to the short commute from Houston to 37th Street. It was exactly 37 short blocks, about 15 minutes via cab and 20 by subway.

I didn't want to move out of Manhattan and was elated to find an apartment on 36th street between 2nd and 3rd Avenue, exactly a block from my job. Unbelievably, it was $800 per month, in a high-rise, 24-hour doorman building. It was called the Murray Hill Crescent, because the building was shaped like a half moon or crescent. The girl who owned the apartment was also from North Carolina and she wanted me in it for that reason - we were both from NC. The one hitch to securing the place was meeting with a residence board and getting approval from them.

My parents came up for the meeting and they co-signed for the lease. Life couldn't get any better than this. I had my own apartment, in mid-town Manhattan, one block from work, five blocks from anything I could ever need and I did it on my own. I had built my castle. I depended on me, I took care of me, and I was all I needed. I thought life should be that simple.

But, I was still empty inside. I was a hollow shell. The outside seemed to be happy and whole to everyone else, but my insides screamed of loneliness and emptiness. I couldn't imagine why my achievements didn't make me feel the way I thought they should: confident, happy, peaceful and whole. I connected those attributes to achievement, things that I did on my own. It would be many years and many bad decisions later before I would know where they truly came from.

Chapter 9
My First True Love

I remember the first time I did heroin. It was nothing like I expected. I was visiting Peg in Rochester, where she attended Sarah Lawrence College. It was about an hour's train ride away. It was always so relaxing and beautiful. Along the way there were trees, and lots of houses to look at. It was much different from the subway, which was underground. In the subway, there was nothing to see except the occasional graffiti that was splayed along the tunnels until reaching the tiled subway stops that were always filthy and scattered with trash.

Peg was in her second or third year at Sarah Lawrence and she loved it. It was and still is a very prestigious school. I found that most of the kids there were spoiled and rich.

Peg had been raised for the most part by her nanny. She told me once that she had no memories of her mother ever taking her to the park or really spending any time with her at all. All of those memories were reserved for her nanny. I think that is why we connected so well. She was psychologically injured and so was I. No matter that we were scarred in different ways, we were both still emotionally damaged and could relate to each other in ways that we couldn't relate to others.

I went to see Peg because she asked me to come to a dorm party that a few of the kids were having. No particular room was specified. It was just kind of spread throughout the building. Me, Peg and one of her friends stayed in Peg's dorm area with the door to the hallway opened most of the night. Her space was connected to the room next door by a shared bathroom. One person per room and they all had a bed and a dresser along with whatever decorations the student brought.

I knew we would be drinking and doing cocaine. That was the standard. This night, however, was unusual. An additional invitee came to the party: heroin.

I had never done or been around heroin before, so I had no idea what to expect. And I really didn't know that the amount of heroin and cocaine I did that night could have potentially killed me.

The kids throwing the party provided the drugs. I can't imagine how much it all cost, but it was obvious that cost didn't matter to them. There was plenty for everyone. After sniffing the first line, they told me that mixing heroin and cocaine is called a speedball. I heard the term before, but never knew exactly what it meant.

They would pour some cocaine on a mirror and then add some heroin to the mixture. The cocaine was rocky and hard, so they used a razor blade to chop it up. Then in a few smooth motions, they slid the razor across the mirror and several lines of white powder would be left, perfectly mixed, about 2 inches long and an eighth of an inch wide. The straw was cut in thirds. Then we took turns snorting one up each nostril throughout the night.

After doing who knows how many speedballs, I felt very nauseous. I spent the next several hours in the bathroom throwing up. I was so violently ill that I could barely get in a breath between each wretch. I was very aware that I could die from asphyxiating on my own vomit. It scared me so badly that I decided I hated heroin. After the episode in the bathroom subsided, I crawled into Peg's bed and cried until I finally fell asleep.

For a time, I was an anti-heroin spokesperson and constantly told Peg that she should stop using it before it killed her. I didn't use heroin again for at least six months.

* * *

Peg moved to 12th Street for the summer break and had a one-bedroom apartment that was decorated in a rock and roll theme, mixed with some oriental accents. It was perfect for our lifestyle. A comfy sofa sat along the wall shared by the kitchen and living room with a pass-through window cut out of the wall above. Posters of her favorite bands hung on the other walls. A couple of chairs sat randomly in the center of the room facing the sofa with a fake sheepskin rug underneath. And there was lots of music to listen to on Peg's stereo. She had Bose speakers that would rattle your frame and she wasn't afraid to crank it up.

Peg and I made plans to go out one Friday night, so I took a cab from my apartment on 36th Street to hers and we were going to walk to the club. When I arrived, I saw Peg had already begun to party. She had scored a bag of heroin and was getting high. I told her how disappointed I was in her and that she really should not be doing that. I noticed that her apartment was a disaster and the cat box was full. I scooped out the litter and picked up some of the beer bottles and trash and threw it away. I loved Peg and was really concerned about her. I knew she was special. She was bright, pretty, and motivated, but emotionally she was damaged, like me.

I didn't expect to hear what she said next, "You know you just did too much when we were at Sarah Lawrence that night."

"What?" I asked, shocked by the abruptness of her comment.

"You did too much. That is why you got so sick. Here just try this little bit," it was literally the size of a match head, "you will love it," she said.

I fought this for a little while but I was never one to not join the party, so I said, "I will try anything twice, just to be sure I did it right."

We didn't make it to the club. Instead, we sat around and listened to music, nodded and talked about nothing. I was content for the first time in a long time. I didn't care to do anything.

I fell in love that night. Heroin felt like a warm blanket, wrapped around me, not allowing anything in to hurt me. If I had to guess what a baby feels like in its mother's womb, it would have to be close to the way heroin made me feel that night; safe, secure, untouchable, perfect, right, warm, and loved.

Chapter 10
Prostitution

The owner of the apartment I rented on 36th Street wanted to sell. The thought crossed my mind to try and buy it. I was making decent money and the asking price wasn't too bad. I loved my apartment and felt so grown up there. I didn't want to leave, but it would have been a stretch for me to make the mortgage payments.

After talking about it with Peg, we decided to move in together. She was going to take a year off from school and work an internship for an independent record label called Earache Records. We looked around and found a place at 400 East 14th Street on the corner of 1st Avenue on the Lower East Side of Manhattan.

I couldn't believe the beauty of the roof deck. At the time, the Lower East Side and Alphabet City were pretty run down, but this building had the most beautiful roof deck I had ever seen. The rooftop was completely boarded with wood planks, the benches matched and were scattered all about with planters attached that had small trees and plants in them. It felt like a little bit of North Carolina in the city. There weren't many places you could go in the city to relax and find peace and quiet.

Her parents rented the place and I paid rent to them. It was a really nice, newly renovated two-bedroom unit. Upon entering, the huge living room really wowed. It had to be about 21 x 11 feet. It was extremely unusual to find an apartment with such large living areas. Not to mention that the bedrooms were a decent size too. The one bathroom had been retiled with a neutral color, and had a single sink, and bathtub, but it was nothing more than a regular, no frills bathroom. The whole place was around 700 square feet and we felt like we were in a castle.

I know that Peg's parents didn't charge me half of the rent, but they never told me how much money that half really was. I paid $700 a month.

Peg's parents bought her all new bedroom furniture when we moved in, so I was able to use what she had left from her old bedroom. All I had on 36th Street was a bed and living room furniture. Our new living room could hold both of our couches and end tables. It didn't look mismatched. My couch was white, so it went with her stuff just fine. Then all of her oriental accessories were placed around the room in appropriate places. I loved it and so did Peg.

Immediately we started throwing parties. Sometimes we would score heroin, but for the first couple of months we just drank, smoked pot and did coke. We had people over all the time, mostly bands that were passing through New York and were affiliated with Earache Records. And as what always happens with bands, groupies and faithful followers were never far behind. So, if the party was at our place, so were all those people and they all crashed on our floor.

It wasn't long before heroin was incorporated into every

party. It quickly became the drug of choice for both Peg and I. In four short months of living at 14th Street, we were addicted.

My downward spiral became more noticeable than Peg's. I missed work several times a month and when I made it to work, I nodded off at my desk. There were times when co-workers would pass by my desk and my face was resting on the keyboard. I jumped up at their subtle throat clearing or paper rattling. I decided I had to do something or I was definitely going to get fired, so I started saving some coke to use in the mornings to help me stay awake while at work. I sniffed it in the bathroom right outside of my bosses' office. I knew he and my co-workers noticed a change in me, but I thought they would just shrug it off as a phase.

No such luck.

"Dana, could you come in my office?" my boss asked from around the corner.

"Yes sir."

"Dana, we have all noticed a huge change in your behavior."

Oh my God, an intervention... He was the only one in the room, but obviously they had all spoken about me.

"Do you have a drinking or drug problem? You're late every day. I smell alcohol on you and we find you with your head down on your desk a lot. I noticed the signs from a designer that used to work here. Dana, you are like family to us and we want to help. You can tell me the truth."

Considering that I had been stealing money from the petty cash fund to help support my habit, I knew that meant I had a problem, so I was honest with him. I really didn't like what I had been doing. Bob was like a second Dad to me, at least while at work and I hated that I was disappointing him. Flashbacks to my childhood ran into my mind and I felt like that little girl who constantly screwed up and disappointed everyone.

"Yes sir. I thought it could be just an occasional thing, but I seem to have gotten addicted. I get very sick when I don't use."

Bob was a wonderful man. He was so understanding and concerned. I couldn't believe I was having this conversation with my boss, but like I said, he was like a second father to me.

"I would like to help you. What can I do?"

I blurted out the first thing that came to mind. "I can go to my sister's house and get clean. I should be ok then." I had no idea if she would even let me come stay with her, but I knew she loved me and I knew she would do what she could if I explained my situation.

"Done. Make your arrangements and I will pay for it. You are like family to us and we want you to get the help you need, but if you come back and are still using, we will have to let you go. Understand?"

"Yes sir," I said, so very grateful for the opportunity of a second chance. "I will get it together, I promise."

That promise would be the first of many broken promises I made when it came to drugs. And from this a new problem arose: How was I going to tell my sister?

I told her once that I was dabbling in heroin, so I decided to be straight forward this time. She didn't hesitate, and told me to come as soon as I could. I told her not to tell my mom and dad because I didn't want to disappoint them. Since I started using heroin, I reduced my contact with them more and more.

I had no idea what a full detox would entail. I knew, however, that the small amount of withdrawals that I experienced when dope was hard to find, made me feel like I would rather die than suffer. I was afraid, but I knew I had to do it. I copped enough dope to get me by on the trip and the first day. I planned on staying for 10 days, plenty of time to get back on track.

* * *

My withdrawals were terrible. It started with nausea. I couldn't eat or drink and if I did, I would throw it right back up. I couldn't sleep. I could close my eyes for 20 or 30 minutes at a time, but I would wake up and feel tormented by the lack of sleep I was enduring. I had cold sweats. My skin felt clammy and I couldn't stop shivering. My diarrhea was so bad that I was scared to leave the bathroom for fear of an accident, of not being able to get to the toilet in time. I had muscle aches; my legs jumped. It was awful. It felt like the nastiest case of the flu imaginable times ten.

On top of the physical withdrawals, my mind was in complete overdrive. I had delusions of stealing a car and driving back to NY to get high. I wanted to figure out a way to find someone in Greenville that sold dope. I didn't know anyone there except my sister, but my mind told me that I should go out and look, anyway. I would have had to walk, because I didn't have a car. At the time, I thought it was the most horrible possible withdrawal anyone could have. I was so wrong. I had no idea that later my withdrawals would make me wish I was dead.

"Why did I ever start using heroin?" I whined to myself, "If I just hadn't done it that first time…"

Since then, my sister has informed me that I was the most dreadful houseguest in the world. She said she would come home from work and see that I had stuff strewn all around the room beside the recliner that had become my body cast: newspaper, empty drink cans, magazines, blankets and pillows. Everything was a complete mess. But eventually, I got clean. I felt ready to face the world.

I went back to New York and just a week or so later, I started using again. I couldn't get heroin off my mind. I went through the worst mental torment. Again, my mind played tricks on me. When thoughts of using crossed my mind, I tried to fight it, but it was no use. I convinced myself that if I just went out and got a bag, and put it in the drawer and didn't use it, that I would be comforted that it was there if I needed it. That sounds ridiculous, but in my state of mind, it was completely logical. The bag would last about five minutes at most in the drawer before I grabbed it and sniffed it right out of the sack with a straw.

Needless to say, I lost my job not long after I returned from North Carolina. I knew it was going to happen, so I tried not let it affect me emotionally. I didn't want to connect with what was happening with Bob, my job, and more importantly, my life.

Immediately, I poured over the classifieds for a new job. I had no money, I was addicted to heroin again, and I lived with Peg whose parents had become concerned that she was addicted to something and considered bringing her home.

I found an ad for a door person at a gentleman's club in the paper. I assumed a gentleman's club was a strip bar. I called the number listed and the girl on the other line told me to come in for an appointment the very next day.

The address she gave didn't look like a strip club. It was an apartment building. I assumed it was just where the hiring took place, so I rang the bell.

"Who is it?"

"Hi, I'm Dana McLawhon. I'm here for my appointment. I called yesterday about the ad in the paper."

The door buzzed.

"Have a seat and Sharon will be right with you."

The building had been remodeled into an office of sorts with a glassed-in receptionist area and there were several doors on each wall. All of them were closed. While I sat and waited, a man came out of one of the rooms, smoothing his hair and looking around suspiciously. Shortly after him, a girl walked out of the same room. She was scantily dressed with heels, at least 4 inches, and looking a bit disheveled. She walked right past me without saying a word and just went into another door as the man left through the door which I just entered.

I remember feeling a little concerned at that moment.

Something didn't quite seem right. *If this is an interview for a strip club, why aren't the offices at the club?* It just didn't fit and I soon found out why.

"Dana?" the voice came out of one of the other doors. "Come on in."

I was in the room for about two minutes before I found out the place was a brothel, not a strip club, and they didn't want a door person, they wanted a call girl. It was almost like she expected me to just know. She started talking like it was an everyday thing.

"We charge $300 for the hour, you pay us $100 for the room and you keep the rest. The hour includes sex, you can charge extra for anything else you consider to be kinky. You have to tip the phone person for scheduling your dates at the end of the night. Tip her good and she will give you the best dates, tip her bad and she will give you the worst dates. It is that simple. Can you be here tomorrow?"

Already feeling a little ill from withdrawals and needing to get back downtown to cop a hit, I considered her proposal. I have already been having sex with men for free and got nothing in return. So, I may as well be getting paid for it. The resolve I had come to years before returned and I decided to, once again, simply not care. I just needed to make some money so I could get high.

"Sure, I will be here. What time?"

Your shift will start at 8pm. Be here about 15 minutes early so we can discuss the rules.

The next night I arrived at 7:45 as she requested. There was a new guy there who wanted to see all the girls and choose for himself.

So, Sharon lined us up. I couldn't believe it, but he chose me. I felt like throwing up.

I must have looked scared out of my wits because one of the other girls came over and said. "Just close your eyes and think of something else. Do you have a condom?"

"No."

"Here, just relax, it will be over soon." Handing me the condom and pointing me towards the door.

Somehow, I was able to disconnect with what I was doing. I just went into a sort of auto-pilot state. The men didn't treat me badly, at least from a prostitute's perspective. But today, I realize that they did treat me badly. They objectified me and used me for their own pleasure, but if I hadn't made the bad decision to get high and to prostitute myself, then they wouldn't have had the opportunity to treat me poorly.

Chapter 11
Homelessness

Snorting heroin ceased to have as much an effect on me as it once did. One little sniff just didn't give me the same warm feeling as it did when I first started using. Snorting took the edge off, but I needed around five or six bags a day to get by. A bag cost $10 and was about the same size as a small packet of salt. So, instead of snorting, I decided I would try to shoot a bag one day with a friend of ours that was staying with Peg and me. I hoped that by shooting heroin, I could use less and save myself some money.

New York City has a program for intravenous drug users, called the Needle Exchange. A junkie can bring in dirty needles, which keep used needles from being thrown out on the street, and exchange them for clean ones. The trade-off was one dirty needle for five clean ones. Our friend was a member there and gave me a clean needle from his stash. He then showed me how to tie-off around my upper arm, hold the belt with my teeth, tap on my arm until a vein popped up and stick the needle in. It amazed me to watch the blood shoot into the shaft of the needle. That was my cue to push in the plunger.

I found out that I am quite ambidextrous, but only when it came to shooting drugs. I could shoot in either arm, depending on where I could find a vein. I never had good veins to begin with, but shooting up every day made them even worse. They would collapse and sometimes I swore they were just hiding.

The instant rush, the small amount needed for a shot, and the immediate relief from withdrawals was amazing to me. I was hooked on shooting. Whenever I shot up, I felt a wave of warmth from my head to my feet. Then I experienced the nod. It was like all my problems disappeared. I entered a realm of nothingness, almost as if I was invisible or non-existent. I wasn't concerned about anything. Whatever bad that had happened to me didn't matter. Shooting heroin made my old resolve not to care about anything easier than ever.

What I didn't realize was that it took more and more dope shooting to get that same high. Going back to sniffing was out of the question. It would cost a fortune. My tolerance level for the drug went sky high. The money I thought I would save by using less was a thing of the past. I surpassed level after level, and was now shooting about $100 per day in heroin and another $100 in coke.

Working at the brothel didn't seem so bad. I made pretty good money and as long as I stayed high, having sex for money didn't bother me. I always had plenty of heroin on me so I could numb myself between clients. The men were nice sometimes. I could always tell if they felt guilty. They tipped better than the ones who didn't care. Once it was over, I could see that look of shame on their faces, and I recognized it. Some of them had an addiction, like me, only theirs was a sex addiction. I just didn't realize it completely until now. At the time, all I was concerned about was getting paid, so I could keep the withdrawals at bay for another day.

Eventually, my habit became so expensive I had to come up with a way to make even more money. The brothel didn't give me enough hours. They only gave me one or two dates a night and only three or four nights per week, I had to do something else. So, I asked the other girls what I could do. One of the girls suggested I work the street. That scared me.

"Don't you have to have a pimp?"

"Not if you go down to 12th Street, that's where the junkies go. Pimps don't hustle down there. Most of those girls are sick. They have HIV and stuff so the pimps don't want nothin' to do with 'em."

"How much do they make?"

"Not much per trick, but they only spend a few minutes each time and they can get another date pretty quick."

I didn't go to 12th Street immediately, but within a couple of weeks, I ran low on dope and needed some cash. So, I walked over and checked it out. The place where the girls hung out was on the same block as Peg's old apartment. I couldn't bring myself to go through with picking up a date…not yet.

I remember once, when Peg lived on 12th Street, a man drove up to me and Peg and asked us to party. We didn't realize it then, but he must have thought we were working girls. We were so naive.

* * *

Peg's mom and dad came up to New York and once they saw how trashed the apartment was and how bad Peg looked and behaved, they packed her up and took her home, immediately. They told me I could stay in the apartment until the lease was up. Since that was only about two more months. I panicked. I was late on the last month's rent and I assured them I would pay. I never did.

Two months went by and I had to get out. I rented a storage room and had a friend help me take my stuff there. My favorite bartender at Finian's Rainbow, "Motor City" James, offered up his couch for me to sleep on for a couple of weeks. He was a blues harmonica player and Motor City was his stage name. He knew I was hooked on heroin and cocaine, but he didn't care because everyone he knew was hooked on something: heroin, coke, alcohol, or pills.

Motor City was not your typical lower east side blues player/bartender. I guess he was around 40 or so at the time. He was extremely laid back, and didn't seem to have an overload of concerns. He wore clothes that your normal, everyday Joe would wear: jeans and button-down striped or plain shirts, tucked in, glasses. A smile was always on his face and he could make you feel right at home with just a nod. He had a genuine spirit about him. He obviously loved people.

I was still working at the brothel, but I was desperate for more money. I walked over to 12th Street from St. Mark's Place, near James' apartment. Twelfth Street is a quaint street, clean and charming. Most of the buildings are brownstones with the exception of the New York University Building on the corner of 12th and 3rd Avenue. A couple of the buildings have an awning that reaches from the front doors to the curb. Later, that would be the place I would wait for customers, or "tricks" as they were called on the streets, when it rained.

There were never many girls on the street at one time. We would walk around 12th Street across to 11th Street and back around, just circling the block. We had to keep moving or the cops would know what we were up to. We made ourselves believe that they didn't have a clue. Looking like broken-down junkies with messed up hair, ill-fitting and dirty clothes, it would have been obvious to the most ignorant person what we were doing. But drugs deceive and delude.

Within minutes, a car pulled over about four yards away. I walked up to the open window, leaned over and the deal was made. I jumped in and we drove off. About 15 minutes later I was back at 12th Street with $60 in my pocket. A couple of minutes later, another car pulled over.

The danger of what I was doing was enough to scare the average person to death, but a heroin addict is hard to scare. I just jumped in and out of cars with men I had never seen before and probably would never see again. I can barely imagine it now.

The most important things to me were heroin and cocaine. I lived for them. Every step I made was focused on getting more and more drugs. My life had become very simple. Make money for drugs, go buy drugs, take drugs, repeat. That was it.

I tried very hard to keep my parents out of the loop when it came to my life at the time. I couldn't admit to them that I was addicted to drugs, prostituting myself and nearly homeless. I called them randomly and tried to portray some semblance of normalcy. They knew better. They had been in touch with Peg's parents and were growing more and more concerned about me. I gave them Motor City's number to try to show that I had a place to live and to comfort them a little, if not to just keep them from knowing the truth about me.

A few months later, Motor City asked me to leave. My parents had been calling him and asking about me. Being that I didn't show up to his apartment sometimes for several days, he couldn't continue to lie for me and field their questions. So, I took what little I had and left.

I was officially homeless, and stopped working at the brothel, which was too far uptown to travel. I made more money on 12th Street anyway. I was 25 years old, homeless, addicted to heroin and cocaine, and a prostitute. Could life get any worse? It's hard to believe, but it did.

Chapter 12

Someone Is Killing Prostitutes on the Lower East Side

The news spread like wildfire. Someone was killing prostitutes on the Lower East Side. All of the street people were talking about it, but it didn't really faze anyone. Business of my kind went on as usual. We had a mission, a purpose, and nothing or no one was going to stop us. Our drugs were more powerful to us than any threat of murder. Besides even if the killer did get us, then we would just be put out of our misery.

There were several of us working girls hanging out on 12th Street when the police came by and rounded us up. They said they had to "…take us in for our own good." The back of the van was filled with drama on the way to the precinct. Everyone was speculating about what was going on.

"They just wanna harass us," one girl complained through a mouth full of deteriorating teeth. Her face was picked at so badly that I couldn't tell the difference between the healed scars and the newly agitated sores. She was definitely a crack addict. That is what they did. They nervously picked at their skin.

"Yeah," agreed another girl who was wearing an outfit she obviously found in a trash bin. The shirt was too small and the pants were way too big. They were held on with a belt that was shredding apart. It all looked pretty normal to me at the time. They looked just like I did.

"I'm gonna offer one of 'em a date and see if they'll let us go," joked another, laughing at something that should have grieved us all.

When we got to the station, we sat handcuffed to the bench next to each other while the police questioned us one by one. They called out one of our names and an officer came over, unlocked the cuffs, and led her to the desk. The room smelled of cigarettes and I wanted one desperately.

Sometimes the cops would let us smoke.

They would say, "Smoke 'em if you got 'em." We all liked those cops.

The interrogation rooms were nothing like the ones you see on TV these days. The police departments in New York City are old, dingy, plaster walled rooms, at least the ones I saw. There were mismatched desks and most of them didn't even have divider walls. The desks were just sitting randomly out in the middle of the room. The only high-tech machinery I ever saw were the finger printing machines that barely worked. They would have to print us over and over again to get it to take.

When they finally called me, I was glad because soon, they would let me go. I was ready to make some money and get high. The withdrawals were already coming on. My skin crawled and I felt a little nauseous. I always got really nervous when I started getting sick, because I wouldn't be able to work.

"Do you know a prostitute by the name of She?" the cop

asked.

"No." I said, knowing full well that I did. All I wanted to do was leave. If I said I knew her, then a whole other can of questions would open. I didn't know anything about her, just in passing on the street really. Then he pulled out a Polaroid picture of a girl. I looked at it for a few seconds before I could really tell what I was looking at. The girl I had known from the streets, who went by the name of She, was mangled, twisted and beaten almost beyond the point of recognition. I noticed in the picture, before he took it away, that a broom had been used to sodomize her.

This was what they were trying to save us from. Some guy was taking prostitutes out and torturing them to death. It was something straight out of a serial killer movie. I should have been scared of working the streets, but I wasn't. As soon as they released me, I went straight out, made some money, and got high. Drugs took away fear, pain, and emotions. I didn't worry about anything else, just getting high. *Besides,* I thought, *it won't happen to me.*

A couple of days later, word on the street was that it wasn't a serial killer that killed She. There was no serial killer at all. She had been taking her johns to a forbidden place. It was the rooftop of the apartment building belonging to one of the biggest Lower East side drug dealers. We couldn't be certain it was true, but I knew that was where he lived and I also knew better than to take my johns there. Word was she had been warned not to go there anymore, but she didn't listen. It was said that they beat her to death as a lesson to us all.

Of all the bad decisions I made, thankfully none of them got me killed, no matter that many times they should have. The life I was living was more dangerous than I even cared to admit. I continued to use drugs and blocked out She's reality and mine. So easily, I could have gotten into a car and never been seen again, or been in the middle of a drug deal gone bad. But for the grace of God, go I.

Of all the people I knew on the streets of New York City, people like me, hers is the only name I remember… "She."

Chapter 13
The Kindness of a Stranger

During that period of my life, I would stay awake for days, three, four, five days at a time. If I wanted or needed to stay up, I would shoot more cocaine. If I wanted to sleep, or had a place to sleep, I would shoot more heroin. It was a vicious cycle, but it served its purpose. I couldn't just fall asleep anytime and anywhere. It was dangerous to sleep on the street but that is where I always was.

Many times, after being awake for days, in need of a place to sleep, I would just walk up behind someone at their apartment building door and follow them in as if I lived there. Or, I would catch the door before it closed all the way and locked. I could then go to the top of the stairs and sleep inside on the landing. There, it was quiet. Rarely did anyone come up there. If someone did come up, I could usually run down the stairs and get out of the building before someone called the cops.

The stairs were a safe place to sleep. I never really slept on the street, even though I was homeless, but I sure slept in a lot of stairwells. I even learned how to break into apartment buildings using a plastic card or by cutting a plastic milk jug into an "L" shape to slide between the door and the lock to jimmy it open. To this day, I am an expert at B&E, breaking and entering. If anyone I know is locked out of their house, I can get them in.

There were a few times when the apartment dwellers called the police on me while I was sleeping. Usually, if I didn't have drugs on me, they would just let me go. A couple of times I got arrested for trespassing and a few other times for trespassing and simple possession. However, sleeping in stairwells was safer than sleeping on the street or in the park. I didn't have to worry about getting hurt.

I also preferred to get high there. It was convenient. When I shot drugs, I needed a place where no one would bother me, especially since my veins were hard to find. It could sometimes take 10-15 minutes to shoot up, depending on how cold it was or how bad my withdrawals were. The cold air made my veins shrink down to nothing and if I was sick, I couldn't keep my hands from shaking long enough to hit the vein.

There were times when I was so sick I had to just stick the needle into the muscle instead of a vein. I wouldn't even try to take the time to find one. It took longer to feel and it didn't have that wonderful rush, but it fixed me and I could always get another shot after I "got straight."

"Getting straight" is junkie slang. It basically meant that once I did my heroin, I could function again. Withdrawals kept me from even the simplest of functions. I couldn't control my bowels. I couldn't eat, talk to people or even stand to be touched. There was one time in the train station that my withdrawals came on so quickly I had yank down my pants before I defecated myself. I was standing behind a huge square column and thankfully no one was around. The withdrawals I was having were tons worse than at my sister's house. This was like nothing I had ever experienced.

I used to say, "If you had the flu and knew that taking a certain medicine would get rid of it, you would take it, right? Well, it's the same with heroin withdrawals. I get sick and I know that dope will make me better, so I take it. That is why it is so hard to detox. You know what will fix you, and so you take it."

I was so afraid of getting sick that I would go to extreme lengths to be sure I didn't. I would go to 12th Street to pick up a date, even when I knew the police were around, or when I knew a trick I robbed was out trying to pick up other girls. I didn't care about the consequences. I just knew there was nothing worse than getting sick and not having any dope.

I remember one day I was starting to get sick. I scored some really potent dope and climbed to the top of a staircase to shoot it. Immediately, I started to "nod." It was so strong that before I knew what was going on, I went from sitting on the top step to tumbling down an entire flight of stairs. My forehead slammed into a concrete wall, and I stopped.

Touching my head, I felt the blood running down my face. I don't remember being scared that I was seriously injured. I just remember thinking that I couldn't knock on a door to get help because I was trespassing. I had to get out of the building. Surely someone heard me fall and would call the police. I had more dope on me and it was so good that I definitely didn't want to get caught with it and have them take it away.

On leaving the building, I was somewhere around 7th Street between Avenue A and B. I walked over to Avenue B with blood running down my face. I could barely see for the crimson flood dripping into my eyes. People were looking at me, but no one stopped to help or ask if I was ok. They just looked at me and kept going.

As I was walking, I noticed a maintenance man that I saw regularly in my daily quests around the lower east side. He was standing outside the building he worked in. He was always nice to me and seemed to look past my obvious dereliction.

"Are you OK?" He asked with intent and concern.

"I am fine; I just need to wipe my face off."

"Come on in," he said pointing to the basement entrance of his building, grabbing my arm as if to help guide me.

"What happened to you? These cuts look pretty bad. You might need to go to the hospital and get some stitches."

"No!" I reacted, "I am fine, really. I just fell down some stairs. It isn't that bad. It will stop bleeding in a minute. Can I just wait a few minutes here and keep some pressure on it?"

"Sure," he said, looking at me, not with pity, but with compassion. "Can I get you anything while we wait?"

"No. Thanks." I felt comfortable in his presence. I knew I didn't owe him anything for helping me. I also knew he wasn't judging me, that he actually cared.

I remember wondering if he knew someone like me or if maybe he used to be on drugs himself and understood. I questioned why people were nice. It was something that I rarely encountered in my life and even though I trusted that he was genuine and not after something, I still speculated as to why he would care about me. How could anyone care about me? I was, in the eyes of many and myself, the scum of the earth.

After about 30 or 45 minutes of keeping pressure on the cut, my head stopped bleeding. I thanked him for helping me and went on my way.

This is probably the only kindness I was ever shown on the actual streets of NY as an addict. I still have the scars on my forehead from that day and when I see them I remember his kindness.

Chapter 14
Lost Gift, Found Heartache

It was almost Christmas and I was so homesick. All I really wanted to do was see my family. So, I called my mom and dad and they told me they would send me a plane ticket to come home. I was happy, but afraid of the way I looked. I knew deep inside they knew I was in trouble, but I didn't want them to see just how bad I was.

At this time, I had a steady trick named "Buddy," who bought me clothes and sometimes put me up in cheap hotels. Buddy owned a gym in Manhattan, lived on Park Avenue, was married and had a really nice black Navigator. He told me he was once a crack head, and understood what I was going through in my life. I knew he did some time in jail for robbery, but he never told me how he got his life back on track.

I called Buddy and asked him to put me up for a few nights, buy me some clothes and take me out to get my hair cut. I told him I was going home for Christmas and he said he would be glad to help. He even gave me enough money to buy some dope for the trip. I didn't ask him for any food money, I would just shoplift something from the corner shop. I loved Pop Tarts and was good at grabbing them off the shelf, placing them under my arm and slipping out of the store. My diet consisted of stolen Pop Tarts and twenty-five cent packs of cookies.

The day of departure came and Buddy drove me to the airport. I had stuffed my bra with four bundles of heroin, which equals 40 individual bags. I shot enough to make sure I didn't need a fix while I was in the airport, and once we took off I went to the bathroom to shoot another bag.

I had enough drugs on me to go to jail for possession with intent to sell. That is a felony offense. Even now thinking about it makes me wonder if I was absolutely insane. I had no common sense, just this unrelenting addiction that controlled me and my every move.

I remember being thankful that the needle I had in my pocket didn't set off the alarm. By the time we were halfway to Greenville, NC, I was so high I couldn't hold my head up. So, I just went to sleep.

"Pitt Greenville Airport, the temperature is a warm 60 degrees," the pilot announced along with some gate information I didn't need.

I grabbed my carry-on, which held all of my stuff and walked off the plane into the small terminal. I didn't think I looked too bad, but I felt as though people were looking sideways at me. I shrugged it off and kept moving.

There they were, my mom, dad and my sister, all waving and looking at me with anticipation. I knew they didn't know what to expect. They knew I was on drugs because of their conversations with Peg's mom and my evasive behavior. They probably wondered what I might do or how I would act. Trying to act normal, as normal as we all could in this situation, we hugged hello and walked to the car.

"So, how are ya?" Selena broke the silence in the car.

"I am good. How are things with you?"

"Good."

I was a difficult person at that time, because I had become more emotionally and mentally unstable than ever before and I could flip out at any minute. I guess they realized that the best way to talk to me was with simple, non-intruding questions. And, they were right.

"Looking forward to Christmas?" Mom asked.

"Yes. I don't have any money for presents, though."

"That's ok, we don't need anything. We will take care of the ones you need to get for anyone else."

"Thanks."

Christmas came and I felt awful for not having any presents for my parents and sister. But the dope I brought with me took away the guilt and I didn't dwell on it. I took so much heroin during my visit, that I found it hard to stay awake. I also realized I wouldn't have enough to last throughout my stay.

Panic ensued. My mind raced at how I was going to get through the days ahead. I imagined the worst: being overwhelmingly sick at my parent's house and they having to tend to me. I wasn't having it. I had to come up with something to fix this problem. Yet, I had no idea where to buy heroin in Greenville, NC.

"Mom, I want to change my flight to go back a bit early, ok?"

"Ok," mom replied obviously brokenhearted. She didn't ask why. We knew we both knew the reason, but neither of us would say it out loud.

I called the airline and changed my flight to leave the next day. I felt such relief that I wouldn't have to worry about withdrawals coming on before I was able to get back to New York. Just the thought of being back there brought a calm that I can't explain.

Sitting on the flight, I looked back at the very few days I was in Greenville. I looked at the pretty, silver watch my parents gave me for Christmas and felt embarrassment and guilt over their love and my failures. So, I went to the washroom and took what I always took to dull the pain. I was well aware of the emotions that I didn't want. I never waited to eradicate myself of those negative feelings. Once back in New York, I didn't think about my trip home again.

I didn't realize it then, but when Selena said she would join us at the airport in Greenville for my return to NY, it was because she thought that would be the last time she would ever see her little sister. I never really knew that she loved me so much. I just assumed that she just lived her life and didn't think about me until I visited Greenville and upset her routine.

* * *

Back on the city streets, I could disappear. It was almost as if I blended in with the sidewalks. People looked past me like I didn't exist and I was happy with that. I was once again invisible and the drugs took away all my ability to care.

The day I came back, I stayed awake all night and when the daylight came I was exhausted. I found a stoop down 13th Street and sat down. I must have nodded off, because when I came to, my purse was strewn out on the sidewalk and my watch was gone. I was so upset! How could I not have felt them take it off? I just knew that watch would be the only thing I had from my family for the rest of my sad existence. I wanted it to be a reminder of them.

I looked down the street and saw my wallet about 100 feet away on the sidewalk. I hoped my beloved watch wouldn't be far from it. I got up, stumbled along picking up items and putting them back in my bag: needles, papers, condoms. I knew I didn't have any money in my wallet, but I did have a half bag of dope in there tucked inside a torn piece of the fabric. That was how I hid my drugs, inside the lining of my wallet, or in the waistband of my jeans. A small slit on the inside of the waistband was the ideal spot for a bag to fit. The police couldn't feel it and they couldn't see the cut in the fabric. It was perfect.

Grabbing my wallet and looking around it for my watch on the ground, I stuck my finger inside one of the pockets to feel for the bag of dope. It was there. I didn't see my watch anywhere. When I looked inside the wallet to see if my ID and other papers were still there, I found a small piece of paper folded neatly behind where my

ID was kept. I opened it. Here's what it read:

My name is Dana McLawhon. My parents are Bud and Judy McLawhon. Their phone number is 252-555-4410. Their address is 4433 Norris Store Rd. Ayden, NC 28513. Please call them if you have found me or in an emergency.

The note was in my Dad's handwriting. He, like my sister, thought they weren't going to see me again. It broke my heart and seeing that note made my need to erase my emotions all the more essential.

Chapter 15

I Am a Felon

There was a feeling of danger in the air on the Lower East Side. My definition of danger and danger to the average citizen were probably polar opposites. Surely I would be considered a danger to the public, but to me, danger meant the stillness in the air, the lack of street people, and the fear in my heart that withdrawals would soon overtake me. Danger meant that the undercover cops were out looking to make arrests.

"Hot" was the term we used when the cops were around.

Junkies would pass each other on the street and say, "Be careful. It's hot out there."

I always risked it; the chance of getting caught, and so did some of the dealers on the lower east side. Even though we knew it was hot out, I needed my dope and they needed to make a sale, so we did what we always did, only we tried to be more careful about it.

I walked down Avenue A and didn't see anyone selling anything, so I cut over to Avenue C on 6th Street. I kept walking toward my favorite bodega on 9th Street and Avenue C. *Oh my God!* I thought as I saw what was going on a block away from me. The police were raiding the little store. My favorite little store. I thought, *I hope my friend isn't working today.* The friend whom I entrusted the worst day of my life to. The day I fled after waking in the apartment of a man I thought was dead. I had nothing illegal on me, so I boldly walked right past and watched as they were arresting the guy that was working that day. It was one of the guys I knew, but not my "friend." *Crap, my store is being busted!*

My suspicion that the undercovers were around was correct. I felt grateful that they were busy with someone else, even though it was someone I knew. So, I continued searching for a fix. Why on Earth did I assume that they were the ONLY undercovers out that day? I had seen plenty of sweeps in my career and this was the mirror image of one. But, that is what the drug does to you. On drugs, whatever you need to believe, you will believe. I believed that they were the only ones out and I wanted my dope.

I walked over on 9th Street and made a left on Avenue B. I got about 2 blocks down and a young man, he couldn't have been more than 20 or 21 years old approached me. He said, "Hey, you know where I can get a $20 bag of coke?"

I asked, "You a cop?"

"Nope."

"Yeah, I can get it." *Cool, I'll buy a $10 bag for him, one for me and get $10 for a bag of heroin.* I said, "$20 now for the coke and $10 when I get back for me."

"Okay."

"It's hot," I warned, "cops are around the corner busting a store, you stay here and I'll be right back, gimme the money."

He handed me a twenty and I went across the street into

another bodega that sold coke and bought 2-dime bags. I stuffed one in my stash spot in the waistband of my pants and put the other in an empty cigarette box. I came out, walked across the street and handed him the box with only half of what he thought he was getting inside.

I said, "Gimme my ten bucks."

He looked inside the box and before I knew it, I was on the ground. He was a cop. It was a sweep and I was on my way to the station. I thought to myself, I'll be out in a few hours; it's just simple possession. No big deal. But, it was a big deal. I was charged with a drug sale, a felony drug sale to be exact. I was going to Riker's Island, the world's largest penal colony.

I remember saying to anyone who would listen, "I was set up! This is not fair! He said he wasn't a cop! He asked me to buy it!" I came up with every reason to be upset and play the victim. I was great at shucking my responsibility and blaming someone else. In my mind, I was a victim…period.

In reality, I was out that day and every day with the full intention of breaking the law. I was looking for drugs, not to mention that I stole $10 worth of drugs from him (had he been an average person), and I was contributing to another person's failure in life (again, had he been an ordinary citizen.) I was in all actuality, a genuine criminal. Every step I took was illegal. Nothing I did was based in legal activity. Not even where I chose to sleep at night.

Chapter 16
Courthouse Chaos

I spent the next couple of days in "the tombs." The tombs are the holding cells in the basement of the courthouse in downtown Manhattan. It stunk down there because most of the people, including me, hadn't showered in a while. We weren't allowed to smoke, so everyone was having nicotine fits which made them even more cranky than normal.

I couldn't believe I made it through shake down with a bag of coke and a needle tucked away in the lining of my clothes. I went into the stainless-steel bathroom and closed the door. It didn't have a hook to lock it, so I had to make sure no one opened the door. The door was smaller than the opening to the doorway and so I stuck my foot out to hold the door closed, while I sat on the toilet and loaded my needle with the coke. I shot it all right there in the holding cell. Time flew by from then on until I started to feel the inevitable withdrawals from a lack of heroin.

"Dana Johnston," they called. I had given them one of my aliases.

Finally! Maybe they will just give me time served.

Handcuffed, I was walked out into the courtroom by a police officer. I saw my parents in the audience and immediately, I started to cry. The shame of the situation, knowing what I must look like, and realizing they knew what was going on was almost too much for me to handle without my drugs to help me cope.

My court appointed lawyer came over to me and said, "Your parents have discussed it with the DA, they will take you home to North Carolina, but you will be on probation down there. Ok?"

"What are my other options?"

"You take your chances on the judge and see what he says. He could very well sentence you to five to ten in Rikers."

"I'll go to North Carolina with them," I said, swallowing what little pride I had.

It was done. I would have to come back to New York for another court date in a few months, but the probation was being set up in North Carolina and I was free to go with my parents.

I immediately began to convince my parents that if I didn't get some dope I would be very ill on the drive home. It was the truth, probably the only truth I told them in quite some time.

To my surprise they agreed to stop and let me get me something. So, we went down to the Lower East Side to cop some heroin. My parents gave me some money and I got out of the car. It crossed my mind to just run, but my conscience talked me out of it. I went up to the apartment where the dealer lived and got some dope and while I was there, I got high.

I came back down about 45 minutes later and my dad was in the foyer of the building. He said he didn't think I was coming out and he was going to go and find me. The look on his face broke my heart.

The ride to North Carolina was quiet. We stopped several times to eat, fuel up and for me to go in a restroom and shoot up. Half way to NC, we booked ourselves into a hotel room to stay the night. The next morning, my parents were loading the car and I was going to get high before we left. My mom walked in the room as I was standing in front of the mirror, shooting up in my neck. She looked horrified. I would have been horrified too if I was her. I finished up, put my supplies back in my purse, and followed her out to the car. We both pretended what just happened didn't really happen. We were becoming masters at ignoring the elephant in the room.

Once we were in North Carolina, my parents arranged detox and rehab for me. There was no way I was going to kick heroin cold turkey. I had to have some help. The detoxes in New York use methadone and I assumed the ones in North Carolina did too, but I was wrong. They didn't. All they gave me was some sleeping pills at night. The rest of the time I was on my own.

I screamed and kicked and paced around. The nurses didn't know what to do with me. I know I was about to drive them crazy. I feel certain they dealt with heroin addicts before, but I was probably more vocal than most. I was definitely more vocal than the other people who were detoxing with me. I begged them to get me something for the pain and nausea. It was obvious they felt bad for me, but they couldn't do anything about it.

I was stuck in North Carolina at a detox center that in my

mind wasn't helping me at all. Not being mandated there by the court, I just walked out without a hassle and started down the street in a city I didn't know, going to a dealer I didn't know, or know how to find, and I had no money in my pocket. The withdrawals and the call of the drug fooled me into thinking I was going to find some dope to make myself better. There was no chance. After walking about a half mile, I was so exhausted and worn out from being dope sick, I turned around and went back. Thankfully, they accepted me without a bunch of red tape.

After seven days in detox, I was sent to a 30-day rehabilitation center. Walter B. Jones was the only rehab in Greenville, NC and it was pleasant. The people there were nice and I was starting to feel a little better. I made up my mind to make it work.

I finished the 30-days with no problems and was looking forward to getting my life back together. I was grateful to my parents for not giving up on me. I really wanted to change my life.

* * *

The day came to go back to court in Manhattan. The drive from Greenville, NC would take us about 11-12 hours. I had been clean for about 3 months, but was beginning to feel the urges to get high more and more the closer we got to New York.

While attending the rehabilitation program, they told us we should tell someone if and when we got feelings to shoot up, so I did.

"Mom and Dad, watch me real close, because I am feeling like I want to get high and I don't want to run away. Please, just watch me closely."

They didn't really understand me as a drug addict or the way the mind of a drug addict works. They decided we would spend the night in New Jersey, because it was away from my old Manhattan hangouts and since I had no money to go anywhere, it should be safe.

The next morning, I was still having the urges, but this time I said nothing to my parents. We arrived at the courthouse and the desire to get high was intense being right in Manhattan. The heroin was calling me.

They called my name. My lawyer told the judge I would be going home with my parents to live in North Carolina and I would not be any more trouble to him.

"OK, time served. I do not want to ever see you in this courtroom again. If I do, I will make an example of you. Understand?"

"Yes sir, I won't be back. I promise."

My parents and I walked out of the courtroom. I felt so free. I told my parents I had to go to the restroom. My Dad said he did too. So, I went in while my mom stayed in the reception area. She couldn't see the women's room or the stairs from where she was sitting.

I struggled mentally with myself in the restroom. I heard in my head, *if you run now, you can go and get some dope and feel so good.* I tried to push the thought out of my mind. But, it came back stronger, almost as if something physically had me by my hand pulling me away from safety. I ran. I don't even think I made a conscious decision this time, I just flew down the stairs and by the time I got to the bottom, my Dad was outside. I ran to jump in a cab. I heard my Dad calling after me.

"Dana!"

I jumped in and told the driver 10th Street and Avenue C. I was going to Candi's apartment, a dealer I knew who would give me credit, to get some coke.

Turning around in the seat, I watched my Dad running behind the cab, calling me, "Dana! Dana!" Tears were running down his face.

I watched him struggling to run behind the cab. He had a couple of hip replacements and he limped a little as a result. I knew it hurt him to run like that, not to mention the emotional hurt I was causing him, yet again. The look on his face was torment for me. All I wanted was for that image to be gone from my mind.

I was sorry for what I had done and I cried all the way to Candi's, but the urge had won. I was going to get high and all my problems and emotions would be gone, at least temporarily. I still hate to remember that image and to think of the way my parents must have felt on the long drive home without me.

Chapter 17
My Bills

I didn't know it at the time, but for a couple of years, my parents had been back and forth from North Carolina, combing the streets looking for me…again. They hung flyers with my picture on it and they were able to enlist the help of two New York City detectives, Officers Bill Burns and Bill Foley.

Unbeknownst to me, after many conversations with my parents, Officer Burns promised them that he would find me and I was now his mission. He was touched by my father's plea and could relate because his brother was also a struggling addict. He spent hours and hours of his off-time looking for me on the Lower East Side.

When I ran away at the courthouse, I broke the agreement I made with the judge, and so he issued a warrant for my arrest. Officers Burns and Foley found me, picked me up on that warrant, took me back downtown to the tombs and left me there.

After having been in the holding cell for two and a half days, I was hand-cuffed and placed in the detainee section to the right of the judge. Withdrawals had set in terribly. My skin was crawling from the touch of my clothes and the voices in the room were echoing in my head. My mind raced with thoughts of escape. *What if I just jump over the bench and run out? When I get up front, I will just turn around and run.* It played out perfectly in my mind, but it never played out in reality. The control that heroin had over me was so strong. It made me consider escaping a New York City courtroom. Sounds ridiculous now… and it was.

The entire courtroom was dark wood paneled and dingy looking. It seemed that everything looked dark and dingy to me lately. It smelled musty and that was making me even more ill. I knew any minute I was going to be sick all over the floor.

The other detainees were just sitting there, handcuffed to the bench with their feet shackled trying to look cool, as if being in jail was cool. Picture some tough guy walking in to the room, in shoes that are still connected with that little plastic band. It's not cool at all.

I hadn't spoken with my lawyer since he came back to the holding cell to discuss our plan of action. At the time, the plan was to plead guilty and spend some time in Rikers Island. I didn't know Bill Burns was out in the audience of the courtroom, nor did my lawyer.

Bill was a well-known detective and knew the DA. He convinced them, both my lawyer and the DA of a different plan. Bill was to take me to detox and after that to a residential treatment facility. The DA and my lawyer agree, and so did the judge.

My lawyer came over and leaned in to me. He quickly stated what he had just learned, "Alright, the judge agreed that Detective Burns will get you admitted into a detox in Queen's and from there he will take you to Daytop Residential Treatment Facility. OK?" His hot breath smelled of coffee, and it made my stomach churn.

I knew that I would get methadone quicker if I went to detox that day, so I promptly said, "Yeah, fine."

"Dana Johnston," the bailiff called.

My lawyer motioned for me to join him in front of the judge. I was almost too weak to walk there on my own.

The judge rattled off the charge, not even sure what it was now, "How do you plead?"

I looked at my lawyer for reassurance and he nodded and breathed with his hot, coffee breath, "Guilty."

So, I repeated, almost under my breath, "Guilty."

Slam! The gavel went down and he sentenced me to complete the detox and be admitted into Daytop Residential Treatment Facility. My head was throbbing with the loud thud of his gavel and it seemed to ring in my head all the way to the detox.

I didn't say much to Bill on the way to Queens. I tried to act as if I was doing him a favor by agreeing to go, like doing time in Rikers Island was no big deal to me. Although I didn't admit it at the time, even to myself, I knew he was truly trying to help me, but humility was not on my list of character traits.

We arrived at the hospital in Queens and I was feeling like I had been hit by a train. My entire body ached and I had no strength at all. All I could think about was how long it would be before I could get a dose of methadone.

Finally, I was upstairs having my vital signs taken, drug

testing done, and getting signed in when Bill noticed that my shoes were just about completely deteriorated and that I had no other clothes except the ratty, dirty, smelly clothes on my back. He said he would be right back and ran out the door.

When he came back, he had a bag full of brand new clothes, a bright white pair of Reebok sneakers, and a load of candy; hard candy, soft candy, chocolate and gum. I knew that the candy would help with the withdrawals and so did he. The nurses wouldn't let me take the candy inside, so I ate a bunch of it right then and handed it over for storing until I checked out.

After Bill left, I was officially in detox...again. Detox is an awful place to be, so awful that it actually seemed worse to me than being on the streets. Of course, it wasn't really that bad, but the physical withdrawals and mental bondage made it seem that way. My mind tricked me into believing that being in the hospital with three meals a day, methadone, hot showers, a bed to sleep in, and clean clothes on my back was worse than where I had just come from: nowhere with nothing, and filthy.

The voice in my head, begging me to check myself out of detox, finally won out after about four days of being there. I went to the desk, got my stuff and left. They gave me one subway token to get to where I was going. Even though I was ordered there by the courts, the nurses were just that, nurses, not guards, they couldn't do anything. They would report it and a warrant would be filed on me, and eventually I would be caught again.

"Where is the closest train station?" I anxiously asked.

"About two blocks down."

I grabbed the token and walked very quickly to the train station. I felt relieved to be out of there, to be free again. It is truly amazing how I believed such a lie. I was not even close to being free. I was more bound by my addiction than ever.

I made my way from Queens to Manhattan and down to the Lower East Side. A battle raged inside me the entire way there. I was glad that I was going to familiar ground. Relieved that I was out of detox, but that little voice within me said, "You were on your way. You really wanted to do it this time. Why did you leave? You can't keep living like this." I ignored that voice as best I could.

I spent the day trying to make enough money to cop some drugs. I don't know why, but there was no money to be made anywhere. I began to get a little nervous and decided I should just find a dealer that I knew would give me credit and ask him to front me a bag or two.

I walked over to Avenue B around Tompkins Square Park and found some dealers there I knew. They all came over to me and I explained my dilemma. One agreed to give me a $20 bag of coke and a $10 bag of heroin on credit to be paid back later that night. It was already getting dark out, so I knew I needed to hurry.

All of a sudden, out of nowhere, a white Caprice Classic skidded to a stop about a foot from where we were standing. The dealers took off in every direction away from me, like I had the plague. I was left standing all alone on the corner.

I was scared at first, until I realized who it was. It was Bill. He had tracked me down and he looked pissed.

Jumping out and grabbing my arm, he yelled, "Get in the car!"

"What?"

"Get in the car! You violated the judge's ruling and you are going back to jail."

On the way to turn me in, I asked Bill how he found me.

He said, "The hospital called and told me you checked yourself out, so I decided to just drive through the Lower East Side once before going home. I spotted the new white sneakers I bought you. They were shining almost as bright as the sun. I knew it was you."

It is really amazing to think that this man who didn't know me before my parents called him would take the time out of his life to try and help me. I had become his burden and he had become my nemesis. He wasn't giving up until I was as I should be. Off the streets and recovered.

Chapter 18
DayTop

Well, I was back at the tombs below the courthouse in Manhattan, and for the first time I was called to the courtroom the very same day.

"Dana Johnston." I was getting used to that name and began to think of it as my real name. I think it was easier to separate my real self from my junkie self.

The officer led me to the courtroom and the judge set my hearing for three months in the future. Meanwhile, I was off to Rikers Island for what would be my longest stay there ever. Furthermore, I would probably be spending a lot more time there after my court date. I had spent three or four days in Rikers previously for simple possession charges and loitering. Then it occurred to me they could possibly ship me upstate to another facility.

I went to Rikers on the bus that afternoon. I was handcuffed to another girl who was on her way to Rikers as well. The ride was so bumpy that by the time we got there, I had bruises on my wrist and she did too.

The bus ride was the time to make buddies. Usually whoever you were handcuffed to would become a friend. I knew that we would go through the intake process together, so I might as well make nice. However, this particular girl didn't feel the same way. She had no interest in chatting with me and she said as much. It seemed like she was mad at the world and I decided not to get in her way.

The first step of intake was the bull pens. There are about twelve bull pens or holding cells that hold around ten girls each, if I remember correctly. We waited there to be taken to the next area, which was strip search. Some girls were able to get cigarettes in to the bull pens, either because they came from another courthouse that allowed smoking in the holding cells or because they were weekend warriors. Weekend warriors did their time on the weekends so they could continue to work during the week. Most of them were pretty nice, the court trusted them to do their time and they were not usually street people. They would share their cigarettes for fear of making enemies.

Strip search was humiliating. They made us strip down to nothing, take a shower in front of them, wash our hair with lice shampoo, and then squat and cough. It was very embarrassing. But, it was my fault I was there, so the shame was of my own making.

Next, we were corralled into the nurse's station. Intake procedures could take up to 24 hours total. We would sleep in the chairs and wait for them to call us. We all whined and complained about our rights and how we were being mistreated. I think most of us believed we were right with our complaints. Our common sense was apparently on hiatus.

The nurses' station was where we moaned and groaned the most, especially if you were a heroin addict. These were the people who wrote the prescriptions for methadone. If you were on a methadone program in the streets, you could get your meth the next day, if not, they had to put the order in and it could take up to four days to get medicated. I was always so scared that I wouldn't be able to keep myself together by the time they medicated me. My nausea and vomiting was so bad, I couldn't even keep a drop of water down, much less the powdery solution of the methadone.

Thinking back, the meth line was the only time that the majority of the women would act like they had any sense. In the food line, in the line to go out to the yard, in the commissary line, everywhere else, there would be fights, but not the meth line. If you acted up there, you were either sent to the back of the line or back to your dorm and you may not get called back later to get your dose.

It's strange how an inanimate substance such as heroin or methadone can hold such control over so many people. It has no brain, emotion or life, yet we were all subservient to it. We did exactly what it "told" us to do.

The next step was individual holding cells. Everyone stayed there until medical testing came back and either your time was served by then or you got sent to GP, General Population, which usually meant the dorms.

The dorms were huge rooms with bunk beds set up in rows down the outer walls and a row or two down the middle. There was a huge shower with six shower heads, no walls between and a row of toilets with the doors removed. Toilet paper had to be requested from the guard's station and so did soap.

Every dorm had a recreation room with a couple of tables, chairs and a TV. My favorite past time was playing Spades in there. It was a fun card game and since bluffing was pretty much allowed, there were never any fights resulting from cheating. It was also played with a partner, so it helped in making friends, especially if you were a good Spades player. And I was good.

After being there for a few weeks I was told that I was going to be detoxed off of the methadone. I didn't make the maintenance program for some reason. So, for the next two months, they lowered my dose until it was down to nothing. I still had withdrawals, but not like what I would have if I went cold turkey.

About two days later I went to court for sentencing. I was still going through withdrawals: not sleeping, diarrhea, and skin crawling, but I could keep the food down I was eating, so I was on the upswing.

The bus to Manhattan leaves around 4:00 am, so we had to be ready by 2:00 am to go to the bull pens and be processed out. The bus was full, so it took us every allotted minute to get processed. Then we were off to court.

"I hope I get time served," said some wishfully.

Others hoped for a drug program. I just hoped I could get back in time for dinner. Bologna and government cheese sandwiches didn't appeal to me and that is what we would get in the tombs. I knew I was going to do time and honestly the break was needed. My mind couldn't talk me into using because I couldn't get my hands on anything while I was locked up. If I had money in my commissary, it would have been different, but no one was taking care of me in jail so I had no choice. For the first time in a long time, my mind was telling me other things than simply 'You need drugs.'

Once in the courtroom, I looked out and there were my parents and Officer Burns again. I started to cry. My lawyer came over to discuss my options.

"Dana, you can go back to Rikers for five years or you can go to DayTop today, mandated, and try to get your life back on track. I strongly urge you to go to DayTop. Officer Burns and your parents will take you there straight from here."

Thinking back on everything now, I have a sneaking suspicion they detoxed me in prison because Bill was working on the outside to get me into DayTop without having to go to a hospital to detox again. My nemesis was actually proving himself to be the angel I needed in my life.

With my eyes full of tears, not only because of my parents and the guilt I felt, but because of the opportunity I was getting, I accepted. The bailiff took off the handcuffs and handed me over to my parents and Bill and we walked out of the courthouse together.

On the way to Far Rockaway, Queens, my dad asked if I was hungry and of course I was, so we stopped at a local pizza joint for lunch. It was the best pizza I had ever eaten. We sat in awkward silence for a while and ate.

Once we got to DayTop, another intake process began. I was

starting to get used to all the questioning and poking and prodding. I was very happy that my parents were there with me.

My mom had always cuddled me when I was growing up, especially when I was upset or down. Today was no different, only now I was a grown woman being cuddled by her mother in a drug program waiting room. I felt safe there in her arms. My dad was on the other side of me and Bill was across the room.

The time came for me to go inside and for them to leave. I actually began to have moments of clarity, as if I could build a brighter future. Too bad my demons had other ideas for me. However, they were kept at bay for the time being, and would stay away for more than a year.

While at Far Rockaway, I met a guy named Rafael. One of the rules was that no one could date anyone else in the program. They said it caused us not to focus on ourselves. How true. Rafael and I were really just friends with each other while we were at Far Rockaway, but we both had deeper feelings for each other. So, when the day came for us to be sent to our permanent housing situations upstate, we hoped we would get sent to the same facility.

We didn't. I was sent to Parksville, NY and he was sent to the Swan Lake facility. We would be apart for a year.

While I was at Parksville, I made huge steps of progress. In the treatment center, everyone had a job. The more you worked your program, the higher up your job would be. I moved up the ladder of success, from general worker, to team leader and finally to coordinator. I was trusted to help interview new people as they came in and I encouraged them to open up and get the help they needed. I even told my counselors that I wanted to become a counselor and they were assisting me to put that plan into motion. Things were going well.

Chapter 19
Good Things Happen to Good People

During my time upstate, my father wrote a letter to the Deputy Commissioner, Edward T. Norris, about Detectives Foley and Burns. He told them my story and how the detectives found me.

The letter read:

Dear Mr. Norris,

I am writing this letter on behalf of my wife and myself. It is not intended to describe in detail the heartache we've been through but rather to give credit to a New York City detective for helping us.

We are from North Carolina and have two children. Our youngest daughter, Dana, is a heroin addict. She became addicted after moving to New York City in 1991 when she was 22 years old. Dana held a good job and did well until May of 1995 when she quit her job and started living the life of an addict.

My wife and I made several trips to New York trying to get her help without success. On some of these trips we were unable to find her.

In May of 1996 we were in New York looking for her. After eight days without finding her, we went to the 17th precinct and met with Detective William Foley. He is a fine person in that he took all of our information and did some checking for us. We left New York without finding Dana, but felt comfort in knowing we could call Detective Foley who seemed to understand and wanted to help.

In November 1997, we first spoke with Detective William H. Burns of the 17th detective squad. According to Detective Burns, he had recently been assigned as the partner of Detective Foley and Foley had told him of our situation with Dana.

Since the day we first spoke with Detective Burns, we feel our prayers are being answered. We have prayed for an angel to intervene in Dana's life and we feel Detective Burns is that angel. He described to us a similar situation with a family member. From our first conversation with him, he has taken a personal interest in helping us. I won't go into all the details of what he has done as it would take several pages. Remember that Detective Burns did all this to help people he had never met.

Detective Burns located our daughter. He arranged for her to be admitted into a detox facility and then an extended rehabilitation program. She is currently in DayTop Village in Parksville, NY.

Most of this work was done on Detective Burns' personal time. On 12/29/97 he spent 16 hours helping Dana on his day off. We know this because he kept us informed by phone during this time. He also provided her with clothes, food and other necessities. In early January, 1998, we went to New York and met Detective Burns. He spent his day off with us getting Dana admitted to the rehabilitation program, DayTop.

Detective Burns has demonstrated the ability to get difficult things accomplished. In seven weeks, he accomplished what we were unable to do in three years. He got Dana off the streets and into a rehabilitation program.

We can only pray that Dana will follow through with her treatment. We know that if she does, she will realize as we do that Detective Burns saved her life.

No matter what Dana's future holds, we'll never forget what Detective Burns has done for us. He is truly a special person.

Yours truly,

JE McLawhon

Commissioner Norris in turn recommended that the New York Daily News honor Detectives Foley and Burns as Hero of the Month. The following is that article that was run in the paper in full:

New York Daily News - New York, N.Y.

Cops Mission of Mercy was the title. The subtitle read, How Two Detectives Saved the Life of an Addict.

Author: PATRICE O'SHAUGHNESSY Daily News Staff Writer

Date: Jun 14, 1998

Copyright Daily News, L.P. Jun 14, 1998

With this account, the Daily News brings back Hero of the Month, a regular feature spotlighting those men and women, police, firefighters and civilians, who go beyond the call of duty to make New York a better place. Detective William Burns picked up the phone in the 17th Precinct Stationhouse on E. 51st St. and listened to a desperate man 492 miles away. In a mellow Southern drawl, the caller poured his heart out about a daughter lost to heroin somewhere in the city. Burns thought of his own parents and their heartbreak over another son's battle with cocaine. He drew hope from his family's experience and told the man in North Carolina on that day in November that he would find the man's daughter Dana and do whatever he could to help.

Burns, 37, made it his personal mission, spending his days off locating Dana and dealing with her legal problems. He and his partner bought her clothes, sneakers and food. They spoke frequently with her parents. It took two months, and sometimes she resisted the help. But Burns fulfilled his promise, and, in the process, a friendship was forged between the third-generation cop raised in Morris Park, the Bronx, and a retired couple from a town of 4,800 in tobacco and cotton country.

Dana has been clean for five months. Whatever the future may hold, her parents will always think of Burns and his partner, Detective William Foley, as "heroes" and "angels."

"These two detectives are truly remarkable people," said the parents, Jesse and Judy, who do not want their last name or hometown published.

"Dana has good days and bad days in her program, but she's made remarkable progress," said Judy.

"Burns saved her life," said Jesse.

"I just feel great they got their daughter back," said Burns, a cop for 15 years.

Dana's parents first told their story to Foley, 34, in May 1996, when they walked into the 17th's squad room. They said their daughter had come to Manhattan in 1991, at 22 years old, worked for a graphic design firm and lived on the East Side.

In May 1995, her taste for heroin growing, she quit her job. She was arrested several times on the lower East Side for drugs and loitering.

"She was addicted to heroin," said Judy, 54. "We were at the end of our rope, and we thought we'd see if they could take a missing persons report."

Foley, a one-time narcotics cop, was moved to help a junkie. He tracked Dana to a flophouse on E. 30th St. and urged her to call her parents. He saw her on Avenue A twice after that, looking progressively worse.

She was arrested for drugs in April 1997 and went back to North Carolina for a month of rehab. In May, she returned to the city for a court date and was put on probation, but she vanished into Alphabet City. Around this time, Burns arrived at the 17th Precinct from the 28th in Harlem, and his new partner, Foley, told him of the dedicated parents.

On Nov. 18, Jesse called the squad room, and Burns spoke to him for two hours. "He was crying, and he wanted to make sure his daughter didn't go to Potter's Field," Burns recalled, shaking his head. "It was like listening to my father back when my brother was snorting coke."

Burns and Foley spent days off visiting drug spots, displaying photos of Dana, a tall, thin woman with a snake-and dagger tattoo and a complexion ravaged by five bags of heroin a day. They found her in Queens on Dec. 29, three days after her 29th birthday, and Burns spent 16 hours with her, scrambling to get her into a treatment program.

"The parents had sent me photos of her when she was young, and I dropped all the pictures on the table in front of her, and she lost it," Burns said. "She had been a beautiful girl. She just got caught up; she was a little Southern girl in the big city."

Dana told Burns she had spent Christmas Eve in an abandoned building in Queens. On Dec. 30, Burns took Dana to Midtown Community Court, where he told Criminal Court Judge Margaret Finerty that he had arranged for the woman to enter Daytop Village, the rehabilitation program that had helped his brother.

Dana was released to Burns' custody, but on Jan. 5 she walked out of the detox unit at Queens Hospital Center.

Burns and Foley found her the next night.

"I spotted these new white Reeboks glowing on the corner of Avenue B and E. 11th St., the sneakers we had bought her," Burns said. "We threw her in the car, and she thought we were bringing her to the hospital. But we took her to Central Booking for a probation violation, and she went to Rikers Island."

Dana then agreed to change her life. On Jan. 12, Burns and Foley took her to lunch at a waterfront restaurant in Howard Beach, Queens, then dropped her off at a Daytop receiving facility. Dana resides in a facility upstate, where she is doing well in a structured setting. She is allowed four phone calls a week. Burns and Foley will join her parents to attend a family day next week.

"Dana just thinks the world of both of the guys," said Judy.

The parents plan to be at a Hero Award ceremony at the Daily News tomorrow, where the detectives will be honored for their extraordinary effort.

"Dana, she knows they're getting the award, and she's really, really pleased about it," her mother said.

"We heard so much about New York not being a warm, receptive place," said Judy. "We did not expect this type of help, and it was really appreciated.

"

Sidebar: A CLOSER LOOK

WILLIAM FOLEY
Age: 34

Family: Father of two

Background: Grew up in Queens Village

Favorite thing about N.Y.: Meeting people from all over the world

Most annoying thing: Noise

Best moment on job: "Getting sworn in; thinking I was going to save the world."

Favorite off-duty activity: Softball, racquetball

WILLIAM (Bill) BURNS
Age: 37

Background: Bronx native

Favorite thing about N.Y.: Restaurants

Most annoying thing: Taxis; all-talk-no-action politicians

Best moment on job: "Following in my father's footsteps."

Hidden talent: Part-time actor in "a lot of independent films."

* * *

My parents were invited to come up to New York and attend the ceremony honoring Foley and Burns. It was just days before my first family day at DayTop. I was so excited to get to see them and both Bills were coming to family day too.

I was beginning to feel proud of myself again, like I was accomplishing something. DayTop was like a little community, a mini-life. Everything was based on real life only it was safe and secure. We woke up in the morning, ate breakfast, went to our assigned jobs or to school, and at night we had groups and activities. The facility was run by us; however, counselors were in charge of overseeing everything. It was a great system and it was supposed to be the best of the best of rehabs.

I gained a lot while at DayTop, most especially I was reminded of what life could be like without drugs. In jail, life was just dreary and all I thought about was dope, but at DayTop, there were things to look forward to and it helped me think of other things besides drugs.

I had to go to court for regular checkups though the year, and my court date had come. One of the available jobs for inpatients was van driver. The counselors picked a trusted person to drive the van for everyone who had court that day. Usually there were four or five of us. The courts scheduled it with DayTop so we could go as a group.

"Time served!"

I had a decision to make. I didn't have to go back to Parksville if I didn't want to. I could just walk out of the courtroom a free woman. But, where would I go? What would I do?

I got back on the bus and went back to Parksville. I liked it there and my realities didn't hurt so bad while around all of those damaged people who were just like me. I was comfortable and happy, even though I knew that my time was coming to an end upstate and soon I would be sent back to Far Rockaway for re-entry into society. I was very afraid of that. The comfort and security I felt upstate would certainly not continue so close to Manhattan.

Chapter 20
The Cycle Continues

After returning to Queens and beginning the re-entry level at DayTop's program, I was doing very well. I was allowed to take a couple of weeks to adjust before having to look for work. I met several times with the vocational counselor and we concluded that I was going to continue in the secretarial field. I didn't take any classes that were offered upstate, and I hadn't committed to the counseling opportunity.

Rafael was sent to the re-entry level from Swan Lake about two weeks before I came down. We reconnected again as friends, but that quickly grew into much more. Dating was still strictly prohibited, so we had to be sneaky. We were allowed to go home on some weekends, but since I didn't have family nearby, I had to use an address of a friend in the program. I would tell them I was staying at her house with her family. No one ever checked up on us unless we didn't return to the facility.

I began looking for work and was still doing well in the program, but my attention had been distracted and I focused more on Rafael than I did my recovery. I never actually confronted my issues with self-esteem and men. So, I applied for several jobs. One was a temporary position at Chase Manhattan Bank. After the interview, I felt positive I would get it and I did.

I loved that job. I made great money and began to put aside money for an apartment. Rafael, however, still had not found a permanent job. He decided to go to school in a program funded by grants for rehabilitating drug addicts. He was learning how to buff floors and was paid a few dollars a day while doing on-the-job training.

I grew tired of being at DayTop and thoughts of leaving entered my mind. Once I let the thoughts in, they would not leave until I left.

Rafael's grandmother was very ill and I would meet Rafael at the hospital in the Bronx several times a week to see her. When she died, the family decided to bury her in Puerto Rico where the rest of their family lived, so he had to leave DayTop to go to the funeral service there. They would not allow him a leave to go for more than two days, but this trip required a week's leave.

I decided this was my opportunity to get out of DayTop too. Rafael's father told him he could move into his grandmother's apartment in the Bronx for the next two months, because he had already paid for the rent. But, after the two months were up he had to find another place. So, we moved in and lived there together. After the two months were over, Rafael and I took up the rent payments.

It wasn't long before I found out I was pregnant, for the third time. Rafael was excited and I was as well. I loved him so much and I couldn't wait for our baby to come. I had scheduled my sonogram appointment at the hospital and after giving them my medical history, they determined it was a high-risk pregnancy. You see, in my years of drug abuse, I contracted Hepatitis C and they needed to watch me a bit closer than most pregnant women. I didn't care, this baby was going to fix all of my problems.

One day while at work, I called Rafael at home. He still did not have a job. He answered the phone and we chatted for a moment, and he hung up. Or at least, he thought he did. I overheard a conversation between him and a woman, in MY apartment. Basically, he said something to the effect of, don't worry about her, she is just my baby mama. I was devastated. He didn't love me and was cheating on me while I was pregnant with his child.

I had made a friend at DayTop and we continued to be friends after we left. Her name was Angela. I told Rafael, after I confronted him about his cheating, that I was going to go and stay with her for a few days. I was very depressed, and knew I could not raise a baby on my own. I decided I would get an abortion.

This time was different. I was further along in my pregnancy than I was the first two times. So, I had to have a procedure done, then come back the following day to complete the abortion. The first day they did a sonogram, and inserted a dilator. They had to dilate the cervix because the baby was too large to remove without dilation. The second day they removed the baby. The fact that I actually did this sickens me to this day. When the procedure was complete, I woke up and began to scream and cry. I screamed, "You killed my baby!! You killed my baby!!" I was way to sober to deal with this reality. They moved me into a room by myself to recuperate and got me out of the clinic as quickly as they could. I could barely breathe I was so upset. The guilt has stayed with me and I do not see it getting better anytime soon.

I told Rafael I had a miscarriage. He didn't believe me. I am sure I wasn't very convincing. I know he could see the guilt on my face. It wasn't long before I would leave work and stop at Finian's Rainbow to have a beer before going home. The thought of what I had done was too much to for me to handle sober. The cycle was back in full swing and I had fallen off the wagon. A couple of weeks later, cocaine was back, then heroin. Rafael had never shot up drugs before until one night he wanted to try it. So, I shot him up. I live with a lot of guilt surrounding that as well.

Eventually, we were not able to pay the rent and he asked his mother if we could move in with her. She said yes and we took what possessions we had to her house and slept in the living room. His mom also used cocaine, so we didn't have to hide what we were doing. Soon after we moved in with her, I lost my job due to my felony. They were going to hire me permanently, but when they ran my prints, the felony popped up.

I started working the streets in Hunt's Point, the Bronx. It was a very rough area. At night in his mother's apartment, we could hear gun shots on the streets right outside. A few times we were scared enough to lie down on the floor and wait until it stopped.

I went down to 12th Street sometimes to work as well. On one of these trips downtown, I met Michael. He was a very meek, Jewish man. He was short, wore eyeglasses and had long graying hair on the sides and was balding on top. He was the hippie type, with tie-dyes, etc. He seemed very nice, and lived right around the corner on 13th Street. So, we made the date and he told me to follow behind him, just far enough to see where he went. After he walked into his building, I walked up and rang the bell, he let me in.

His apartment was in the basement, and he owned another apartment upstairs on the 2nd or 3rd floor. I never got to see that one, his wife lived there. She had some sort of germ-phobia and he wasn't allowed to live there with her anymore. He still took care of her, but he picked up working girls to satisfy himself. He wasn't worried about her ever seeing him with one of the girls. She never left their apartment upstairs.

Michael talked to me about getting clean and quitting my working girl lifestyle. It didn't take me long to realize he had developed feelings for me and I was going to take full advantage of that fact.

Rafael and I had to leave his mother's apartment because she was getting evicted and his father said he could live with him, but I couldn't. So, I had to find other arrangements. Michael became my other arrangement.

Chapter 21

My Non-Heroic Account of September 11, 2001

He let me move in and said that he would take care of me as long as I didn't work the streets anymore. Of course, I agreed. I told him how much money it would cost for me to keep my drug habits and he agreed to pay it with one condition, I would try to get on a methadone maintenance program.

I kept my end of the bargain, but told him that I would need to continue to use cocaine for a while until I could wean myself off. He agreed.

One day, Michael mentioned to me that he was saving some cash aside for a rainy day, which his wife didn't know about. He wouldn't immediately tell me where it was, so I began to devise a scheme to make him tell me where he had hidden it.

I made him think I was falling in love with him and that I wanted us to trust each other. I told him I had quit the streets for him and even quit heroin for him.

"How do you expect me to trust you if you don't trust me?" I asked, all the while manipulating away at him.

He told me there was about $3000 in the drawer, right below the bed, and that he would be adding to it weekly. For several months, I ignored the fact that all that cash was there. I wanted the sum to build up, and then I would take it and run off with Rafael. We still saw each other and kept in close contact. I kept him posted on the money situation and he waited with me for the undetermined day.

Around this same time, the terrorist attack on September 11, 2001 happened.

I woke up that morning around 8:30am, got dressed and went outside to catch a cab to the methadone clinic on 25th Street and 2nd Avenue.

While traveling uptown on 3rd Avenue, which goes two ways, I passed a bunch of ambulances going downtown. It seemed nothing out of the ordinary. There were always emergency vehicles around Manhattan. I didn't bother to look behind me. Had I looked, I would have seen the Trade Center on fire about 25 or so blocks behind me.

Once I arrived at the clinic, the nurses had just heard about the attack and turned on their television. I watched the second Trade Center get hit by another plane while I was standing in line to get my daily dose of methadone. It felt as though I was watching a movie. As a matter of fact, I thought I was watching a movie for a minute or two. I didn't realize what was happening, as I am sure most people didn't. After mentally catching up, I thought to myself *That was no accident.*

I was in New York City when the Trade Centers were hit, but I did nothing heroic. I was my same selfish self, just looking after me. I noticed, however, that this city that seemed to shun me for so long quickly became a very friendly place. People were nice to each other and concerned about each other. I tried to show concern for people, even though my own life was in shambles.

There was a girl who lived in the building I was staying in; whose school was not very far from ground zero. She attended an art school of some sort. She sat on the stoop outside one day smoking a cigarette, so I joined her. By this time, I was beginning to look a little more like a normal person, not a street person. She seemed upset about something.

"Hi, my name is Dana. What's the matter, are you okay?"

"Yeah. My name's..." She said her name, but I can't remember it now. "I keep having dreams of that day," she said. It was just a couple of days after the attacks.

"What do ya mean?" I asked.

She told me about the school she was in and that she had a perfect view of the trade centers that day. I had not heard about the people jumping from the burning buildings yet. She saw them jumping, one after the other. She was traumatized by the memories of it. We talked for a little while and she told me she was a painter.

"Paint it," I said. "Paint it and maybe then it will be out of your mind."

"I wanted to paint it since it happened, but I can't make myself do it." She told me she hadn't slept in days.

I never saw her again, even though she lived in the same building I did. Strange city, this New York.

Chapter 22
The Beginning of Change

Today is the day, I thought, *I can't wait any longer.* Five thousand dollars had built up in Michael's drawer and that much money was too big a temptation to pass up. I could barely stand living with him anymore, acting like I really loved him. This was my ticket out.

Michael went out to teach a piano lesson uptown and I went to the clinic for my daily dose of methadone. When I came back, the maintenance man for our building was outside and I asked him, "Have you seen Michael?"

"No, not today."

Great, I thought, *I'll go in and grab my stuff and the money and go.* That is just what I did. My heart was racing and my face had guilt written all over it. I ran out of the apartment, not closing the door all the way, out of the building and over to the Avenue to catch a cab. I took the cab straight to the Bronx.

I called Rafael, told him where to meet me, bought a bunch of drugs and got a room at a seedy motel. We locked ourselves away until we needed to cop some more drugs.

It is kind of hard to believe, but I had convinced myself that the $5000 would get us set up in an apartment long enough to find a job and get us on our feet. It didn't cross my mind that we were addicts and with addicts the best laid plans were usually deceptive and always un-accomplishable. I had stolen a bunch of money, surely the police would be looking for me, and there was no way anyone would hire us the way we looked.

The money was all gone in about six days. Welcome back to life as I had come to know it: homeless, addicted to drugs, and prostituting myself for drug money.

The apartment of Rafael's mother was still vacant and we still had a key. So, we went there to sleep and made sure we were out during the day. It never seemed to bother us that roaches had infested the kitchen and living areas. When we would light cigarettes on the stove, the roaches would frantically scurry out from the burners and into other cracks and crevices.

One morning, we overslept and were wakened by banging on the door followed by, "This is the police, open the door!"

"Man, we gotta get outta here," Rafael whispered. "The fire escape."

He pushed the window up and looked out. The police car was there, but no cops were on the street.

First, he crawled out and then I did, closing the window behind me. We ran down the fire escape and knocked on a second-floor window. Rafael knew the old lady who lived there and she let us crawl in the window and go out her front door.

We watched from up the block as the police came out of the building and left. We realized we could keep staying there now as long as they thought that it was vacant. So, we continued to stay there.

Several weeks later, the police finally caught up with me and arrested me on a warrant for robbery. Michael pressed charges. My twisted mind thought that he wouldn't for some crazy reason.

I was back at the tombs…again. I plead not guilty and they set my court date for a month away. They wasted no time in getting me to Rikers. My methadone prescription was still in effect, so I immediately got medicated, however, I told them to detox me. I was so sick and tired of my life. I don't think I really knew the magnitude of that decision, nor the doors that would open as a result.

My court date came and went. I got six months for larceny. No Bill, no parents in the courtroom waiting to whisk me off to detox or a rehab program or to NC. I was alone, all alone. I was in charge of myself and I had to do something right…for once.

* * *

This will be the last time I'll ever see the inside of Rikers Island! I believed this statement every time I said it. I guess this would make the 5th or 6th time I had been there. I truly meant it and had every intension of it being true. But after a few days inside, all I could think about was getting out, finding Rafael, getting some dope, and getting high.

I was housed in a dorm again and the Corrections Department afforded us three telephones per dorm. Needless to say, this created issues between the inmates. Someone was always on the phone when someone else wanted to use it. There were arguments and sometimes fights.

I would call my family collect almost every day. When I was outside on the street, I would rarely call and then only for money. I'm sure they didn't know which they preferred. Collect calls from jail are very, very expensive, but at least they knew where I was and that I was alive.

For the past year or so, every time I called my sister for money, she would tell me about this God that could make me new. I always thought she was crazy. I thought nothing or no one could change me and take away all the things I had done. I was a horrible person, I was defective, I had done and seen things that I could never be forgiven for. Deep down though, I knew she wasn't crazy. This God had changed her and her husband. This was an incredible feat, and the change in them over the last year was very obvious to me. But I didn't think He could change me.

Well, on one particular day, I was feeling especially upset with how my life had been going. I felt that I wanted to change, but I had no idea how to accomplish change. All I knew was my sister had been telling me about her God. She said He could change me.

I needed Him. I knew it, but I didn't know how to reach Him. I called my sister, collect of course. I told her I was confused. How do I "find" God? How do I "get" Jesus? I really wanted to know. She tried to explain that I have to believe in my heart. *How do you believe something in your heart?*

We talked for a while and I know she was getting as frustrated with me as I was getting with her. I really couldn't wrap my mind around "faith." I always needed proof for everything. This was no different.

For some reason, I asked her to pray with me. She said a lot of words to this God. She spoke them out loud. I don't remember what she said now, but I do know that this was the beginning of a real turning point in my life.

After she prayed, I hung up the phone, feeling confused. Still, I did not fully believe. Even though I was confused, I was finally listening to what my sister had to say about her God and I realized that I needed Him. The rebellious spirit in me was not yet dead, but he was definitely on his way out. He would only live in me for another four months.

Chapter 23
A New Life

In November 2002, my time was served. I waited to be processed out of Rikers, with only the clothes on my back and a couple of items in a bag. One of the girls in my dorm gave me a shirt and some pants to take with me. She knew I was being released into homelessness and I had no clothes to change into.

I had not quite completed the medical portion of the detox and was feeling very, very ill, but I made up my mind not to use any heroin. I need a place to stay and making money with prostitution was not an option if I was not going to numb myself with drugs. I contacted a friend I knew in the Bronx and he hooked me up with a girl I could stay with for free until I got on my feet.

Arriving at the address he gave me, I felt strangely uncomfortable. It looked like a normal apartment, but once inside and talking with the girl, I realized she was a drug addict and was high on crack. *Nope, this is gonna ruin everything!* I thought. I wanted to make my newfound recovery work. I wasn't into smoking crack but the atmosphere would surely lead me back to heroin.

The girl convinced me to try crack with her a couple of days later. I tried it and immediately knew I couldn't stay there with her any longer. I had been out of jail for about a week and I already started using something. *Will this ever end?*

I decided to check into a detox until I could figure something out. Since I hadn't been using drugs, I thought I better get a bag of dope so I could have a dirty urine test. They won't admit you if you don't have drugs in your system.

My plan worked. I was in the detox, safe once again, but since I came in as a heroin addict, I had to take methadone. Of course, the addict in me didn't fight it and I could easily justify it because they would wean me off in the time I would be there.

I contacted my parents and told them where I was and that I would love to come home for Christmas in a couple of weeks.

"Sure, Dana, we can get you a ticket. Round-trip?"

"Yes. See ya then."

I stayed in the detox for the following couple of weeks and got myself back on methadone. I hadn't completely finished kicking methadone in jail and I was already getting myself hooked again. No matter, I was still going home, with no safety net. I was determined. *I will take no drugs home with me this time.*

* * *

My flight was leaving on my 33rd birthday, December 26, and I would be able to spend the day with my family. I was thankful that Christmas had passed and the pressure of not having gifts wouldn't be so bad, however, they still had gifts for me plus birthday gifts. We always made a big deal out of birthdays.

I got off the plane feeling pretty good about the way I looked, but I was wearing jeans that were way too tight, a dingy shirt and a pair of Nike's that I was very proud of. I must have stolen them from a store, because I could never have afforded them. My hair was very long and shaggy, and I had on ninety-nine cent super dark lipstick. I tried to look presentable, and I thought I did, but in reality, I looked homeless, because I was.

The ride to my parent's house was the same as before. Everyone tried to be careful about what they said and how they said it. It was awkward, but when we got home, there was a birthday cake, some presents and my favorite dinner: lasagna. We ate and talked and I opened presents, my favorite. I still love presents.

The withdrawals from the methadone were starting to kick up. Methadone will hold off withdrawals for a few days before you start to feel sick. It had been about three days and I was finding it hard to sleep at night and my legs would kick really bad, I couldn't control them. I had diarrhea, but I wasn't throwing up. At least I could eat. I told my mom what I had done and she coddled me like she did when I was a kid. It was safe there with her caring for me.

A few days went by and my mom came to me in the kitchen, "Dana, you know you are welcome to stay here if you want to."

"Stay here?"

"Yeah, you can stay here, you know, not go back to New York. But, there will be some conditions."

"Like what?"

"Like, you can't use drugs, you have to get a job and you

have to go to church. You can go with us or you can go with your sister, but you have to go every time we go."

"How often do you go?" I asked, confused that it might be more than Sunday mornings.

"Sunday morning, Sunday night and Wednesday night."

Oh my God! I thought. *That is way too much.* But, I really had no choice. I didn't have anywhere to go in New York, and I didn't want to use anymore. The voice in my head kept saying, *You are a survivor. Go back to New York. You will be fine.*

Shutting off the voice, I considered my options and said, "Ok, I'll give it a shot, but can I keep my return ticket in case I change my mind?"

"Sure."

"Fine, I will go to Selena's church." I wanted to rebel a bit more, so I chose to go to my sister's church instead of with my parents. Such a childish thing to do at 33 years old.

It was settled; I would live with my parents in Greenville and go to church with my sister, three times a week. They even offered me an opportunity to make some money by helping them with their wallpaper hanging business. I would apply the paste to the paper for them.

* * *

I guess I could only be compared to a kid with ants in her pants. I went to church with my sister. I believe it was the first time I had been in a church in at least 24 or 25 years. Only this time, I was withdrawing from methadone and was truly unable to sit still. I was at best another month or two away from any kind of normalcy, whatever that meant. I hadn't been "normal" in a very long time.

I must have gotten up from the pew 10 or 15 times during the service. I would go to the bathroom, go outside to smoke a cigarette, or I would just pace the hallway outside the sanctuary. My sister was embarrassed that everyone could see me coming and going so much. She should have known better than to perch me right up on the front row. I hadn't listened to anything the preacher said for the last hour. When I returned from the bathroom or outside or wherever I had been, I sat down...again. I didn't know what was about to happen, nor did my sister. But, as soon as I sat down that last time, Preacher Van asked a question of the congregation and it was the first thing I heard all night.

He asked, "If you were to die tonight on your way home, do you know 100% that you would go to heaven? All eyes closed."

I thought to myself, *No, I know I am not going to heaven. I will be going directly to hell.* For the first time all night, I was still.

Then he asked, "Would you like to know 100% that if you died tonight you would go to heaven? If so, raise your hand."

I thought, *Of course I would want to know that, who in their right mind wouldn't?* I raised my hand. Everyone's eyes were supposed to be closed, so my sister knew nothing of what just happened.

Then he said, "If you raised your hand, I want you to get up and walk up here to the altar."

I jammed my elbow into my sister's side and said, "So, you comin' with me?"

She looked at me thoroughly shocked, but quickly jumped to her feet and walked with me the few steps to the altar.

Preacher Van called on his sister, Diane Bridgman Thomas, the most wonderful woman in the world, to take me to a prayer room and pray with me. Selena came with me for moral support. I have to admit I was a little scared. I wasn't sure what hocus pocus was getting ready to go down in that room.

I met Jesus Christ that night. I didn't see Him in person, but I could see Him in Mrs. Diane's face and in my sister's face. Selena held my hand and Mrs. Diane prayed with me. She asked me to repeat the words she said. So, I did.

I didn't notice anything different immediately. My sister beamed the entire ride home and I just sat and wondered what could possibly come from just repeating some words. I was a little confused, I knew I felt something when I got up to go to the altar, like a tug inside, and now I had this other sensation. It took me a little while to figure out exactly what it was, turns out, it was hope. I had hope within me. I hadn't felt that feeling in a very long time. Not knowing what to expect or exactly what was happening, God had taken that tiny mustard seed of faith and He had plans to use it.

Later a friend of my sister said she had watched me the entire service. Every time I got up and went out of the sanctuary, it was as if the devil, himself, was dragging me out the door. But every time I would come back in Christ, Himself, was dragging me back to my seat. A true battle of Good vs evil.

Over the few weeks prior, I had been experiencing withdrawals, not being able to sleep, eat, sit still, focus on anything or be nice to anyone. But that night, the night I accepted Christ as my Lord, I went right to sleep. I didn't realize it until I woke up of course, but all of my withdrawal symptoms were gone. It was a miracle. A miracle I certainly was not expecting. That is the only thing I could call it. I had suffered withdrawals before, many times, and they don't just up and go away overnight. They get less and less miserable over a couple of months' time. This was definitely a miracle. The first of many miracles to come.

I was clearly made new. It felt amazing.

Chapter 24
A Counseling Session/Interview

Since the day I met Jesus, I have had absolutely no desire to get high or drink. God delivered me when I made the decision to hand my life over to Him and I haven't looked back. As I write this, it really seems as if I am writing about someone else's life. The Bible says that my transgressions have been removed from me as far as the east is from the west. Removed so far away that it doesn't even feel like any of that was me.

I made a lot of bad decisions in my life time, and they led me down a road I never intentionally wanted to go down. It started with what seemed to be small, insignificant decisions at the time, a white lie to my parents, smoking a cigarette or taking a sip of beer, allowing myself to go beyond what my moral compass said was ok with a boy. But, these decisions were able to grow in significance without red flagging my sense of wrong and right, because I allowed them to grow at small integrals. Each step was little; however, the moral and spiritual distance I traveled was huge, compared to the beginning rebellion which started it all.

I found it astounding that the simple decision, to admit my sins, to believe Jesus Christ died for my sins, and that He is the Son of God, would change me so completely. What could I have avoided if I had stuck with that decision long ago at age 13? I look back and see a girl who could have been anything she wanted, but she made really bad decisions in life. Thankfully, my God is a God of new beginnings. I got a do-over! Do-overs are awesome! I made ONE good decision, finally.

I have a new outlook now. Rooms don't look dark and dingy to me anymore. I don't feel less than others anymore. How could I possibly feel less than others and know that I am so precious to God that He sent His only Son to die for me? And at the same time, how could I not tell people, who need to hear it, what He did for me? What He did for me, he also did for them, they just have to accept His gift.

I am also amazed that the miracles didn't stop there. Since the day that I first truly believed, He has not stopped blessing me nor stopped leading me in His will. I helped my parents with the wallpaper business while I looked for another job. I thought no one would ever hire me because of the felony on my record, but all things are possible with God.

I answered two ads in the classified section of the *Daily Reflector*, our local paper. One was for a temporary agency and the other was for a secretarial position at an undisclosed business. I received a call from the temporary agency and went down for an interview. It turned out that my sister knew the owner and she was prepared to send me on some jobs as soon as a suitable one came up. I was overjoyed. *Great, I can get myself back on my feet and work toward buying a car.*

While I was gone, my mother took a phone message for me from the other employer to whom, I had sent my resume. She learned the position was for a church secretary at a local church. I called them when I got home, and scheduled an interview for the next day.

The next morning, my sister offered to take me to the church for the interview. She told me not to smoke before the interview, because they would smell it on me. Even though I had been delivered from drugs and alcohol, I still had an addiction to cigarettes. I didn't understand or even wonder why I still had this addiction. But, I had to smoke before the interview. I was too nervous not to smoke, however I tried very hard not to let the smoke get on me.

Selena dropped me off and said she would be back in an hour. I took a deep breath and walked in the office. The secretary was nice. She shook my hand and told me to go right in.

"Hi, I'm Dana McLawhon, I'm here to interview for the secretarial position."

"Sure, have a seat. I am Pastor Brafford."

"Nice to meet you." I said.

"You too. Um, Dana?" He said with question in his voice.

"Yes?"

"Tell me about yourself."

That was it. I don't know what got into me, but I told him about myself. I couldn't help it. He just asked me a simple question and I spilled the beans. I mean ALL the beans. I confessed my life to him as tears poured down my face.

"Have you been forgiven?"

"Yes sir. I got saved a few weeks ago and have been a completely new person ever since. I am so sorry for crying so much, I hope you understand."

"Don't worry about it. Now, the reason I wanted to interview you was because I saw on your resume that you worked in New York City and I just assumed that you would be tough skinned and able to handle a lot of people. You have to work with a lot of people here. Do you think you can handle it?"

"Yes sir, I do. And I am a quick learner."

The interview went on from that point with all of the basic interview material. He went over the job description with me and asked if there was anything I thought I would find too difficult. I didn't see anything that stuck out to me. And it was over.

"Ok, thank you for coming in Dana. We will be in touch. By the way, do you smoke?"

"Yes sir, but I assure you, I won't smoke here."

I left feeling better than I did when I went in, but I knew there was no way he was going to hire me. I was a felon. I had been clean for a total of about a month, I cried throughout my interview, plus, I was a smoker. There was just no way he would hire me.

A week went by and I heard nothing. My parents always taught me to be aggressive when looking for work. When my Dad was trying to get a job at DuPont at 18 years of age, he sat out on the stoop of the building every day until they finally agreed to interview him. So, I called the church, just to let them know I was still interested. All they could do was say no.

"First Pentecostal Holiness Church, this is Paula, can I help you?"

"Yes, this is Dana McLawhon, I was just wondering if the secretarial position had been filled and if not, I want you to know that I am still interested."

"Can you hold please?"

"Yes, ma'am," I just knew they were going to tell me it had been filled. I thought to myself, *Oh, just hang up, you embarrassed yourself enough with all that crying you did.*

"Dana?" It was a male voice on the other end.

"Yes sir."

"This is Pastor Brafford, I have prayed about this for several days and I have reached a decision."

Silence.

"Yes?" I said in a defeated voice, with just a glimmer of hope in the question.

"You are a part of that decision. Can you start next week?"

"Really?" I said almost too eagerly. "I mean, really," a lot cooler this time.

"Yes, can you start next Monday?"

"Of course, I will be there, what time?"

"8 o'clock am," he said.

"Yes, I will be there, thank you so much!"

"Mom, Dad, guess what?" I shouted to the other end of the

house. "I got the job!"

Chapter 25
How Great Is My God

I was working at the church for almost a year. Still living with my parents and paying off a car they purchased and allowed me to make payments on. It was a cute car, a red 1994 Mitsubishi Eclipse. I liked it, because it reminded me of my 1975 red Datsun 280Z. It wasn't the same, but it was as close as I was going to get.

I was doing very well in my new Christian walk. I didn't mind getting up early and going to work. I was so blessed to be at a church with people who love God. The Pastor included me in the staff meetings and welcomed my input. It made me feel significant and valuable, but I was still extremely lonely.

I didn't have many friends. I assumed it was because I wasn't the best conversationalist. My life revolved for so long around drugs and prostitution that I didn't have much normal subject matter to talk about. I no longer had the cycle of *make money, buy drugs, repeat.*

I prayed one day on the way to work for God to give me something to talk to people about. I asked Him to fill my life with things that I could share with other people. Well, you need be careful what you ask for with God, because He just might give it to you. The next six months of my life were a whirlwind.

* * *

I went on several dates that I found from the dating ads I placed on various Christian singles websites. Most of the dates were what you would expect: strange people who lied in their ads. My name is Blah and I am 34, unmarried, and faithful to God. However, their name wasn't Blah. Instead, they were 44 and married, which proved that the rest of their description was also a lie. Not all men were liars, but most were not 100% truthfully represented. However, I wanted a husband and time was tick, tick, ticking away.

One day I was at the office, all alone, working and surfing the web as I sometimes liked to do, and pop, a Yahoo Instant Message appeared on my monitor. The screen name may as well have been Myfuturehusband2004.

"Hi," myfuturehusband2004 wrote.

"Who is this?" I asked.

"Mark"

"Hi," I said.

Immediately I checked out his Yahoo profile. No crazy stuff. No single but gay, no interest in the occult was listed. Great, I thought. His picture was also very nice. He had dark hair. I always loved dark hair, brown eyes and a smile that seemed to say, *I am laid back and easy to get along with.* This guy might just be a good one.

We chatted online for a while and a couple of days later I gave him my cell phone number. He called me at lunch and invited me on a date. We set it up to meet at Chili's Restaurant, a very public place.

Funny how I was worried about meeting a guy I didn't know for dinner, after all of the stranger's cars I jumped in and out of in New York. Another miracle, I was finally concerned about my own well-being. We met in a public place in separate cars.

After dinner at Chili's, we walked over to Barnes and Noble for a cup of coffee and we sat and chatted. It was pouring down rain outside, so after coffee, we stood outside under the awning and talked some more. I was really starting to like him.

I decided that I wasn't going to waste my time or his and after talking for a while I said, "Well, I am looking for a husband." This came out at a point in the conversation when we were discussing our dreams or life wants. I have always been one to just say what I felt or what I wanted. This wasn't always a good thing.

"Um, I'm not really looking for anything serious," he said, and we continued to talk about other things.

I thought to myself, *I'm glad I won't be wasting my time on him then. I like him but I am not just looking to date around.*

When I got home, I told my mom that I didn't think I would be hearing from him and I told her what I said and what he said. She just gave me that same old look. You know that, *well that is just Dana* look.

The next day, my phone rang. It was Mark, brave soul that he is, asked me out on another date. Then, about two weeks later, while out and about, we stopped at Sonic to get a snack. I told him I had some things to tell him. I told him all about my past. Everything. He shrugged and said, "So? You don't do any of that stuff now do you?"

"No"

"Ok, well then, do you want some ice cream?" and that was that.

At the time, Mark was an Emergency Manager for the state of North Carolina. One day he called to tell me he would be interviewed on TV that evening about Hurricane Isabel. My parents and I were ready to watch. This would be the first time my parents saw Mark. My mom said he was handsome and my father seemed impressed with his professionalism.

About three days later, I invited Mark to come over and meet my parents. Forgetting my father actually has a sense of humor when I am not acting like a fool, it had been a while since I had witnessed it personally, he answered the door and said, "Hi Mark, nice to meet you. Wow, you look a lot better on TV than you do in person."

My jaw dropped and I looked at my mom, who rolled her eyes, she was more used to my dad's shenanigans than I was. Mark laughed, I breathed a sigh of relief, and started laughing too.

When it came time for Mark to go home, my father, ever the funny man, said, "Nice to meet you Mike. Hope to see you again."

Turning bright red, I immediately said, "He is kidding…he knows your name. DAD!!! Stop it!" All in all, it was a good night.

About a month or so after that, we went to Virginia and I met Mark's children from a previous marriage. I liked them. A lot. They were very sweet. Chad has his father's dry sense of humor. And Che', the princess, is beautiful and had this adorable little voice.

While in Virginia meeting the kids, Mark asked them what

they thought about us getting married. They had no objections and after another month went by, Mark and I became engaged. We set a date of March 6, 2004 and that was only three months away.

Oh, did I mention that Mark was in the Air Force for ten years. He was an MP. Yes, Military Police. I love to tell people that, because I was a criminal and he was a cop. Here we are dating…and eventually get married. God has a sense of humor too.

There was a small problem in my fairytale though. Mark had two children and he was not able to father anymore children. I really wanted to have children. I think I felt as if it would be a sign of God's forgiveness to me for all I had done in my life. Especially concerning the abortions. However, Mark was pretty adamant about not wanting anymore children. I had a conversation with my sister about this. I will always remember what she told me.

"If you know that Mark is the man God has for you, then He will either put it in Mark's heart to have more children, or he will take the desire out of your heart."

These words made so much sense to me. I know that my God, who was blessing me, had a plan for my entire life, not just a husband, or just a job, he had a plan for EVERYTHING.

I never felt peace like that about something in my entire life. I didn't know what the plan was, but I was at peace about it. I had given it to God. He was going to handle it for me.

Next item on the agenda was to find a house. I refused to rent and pay someone else's mortgage. I must have still been a little crazy, because I didn't have any money for a house. I had a job, but nothing saved. Nevertheless, I refused to rent. Mark patiently endured all of my craziness. He is a saint. Yet another miracle. Remember Mark was in the Air Force, so we had access to a VA loan.

We found a lot and a house plan that we liked, one we could afford. With Mark's VA credentials, we didn't have to have any money down and we began building a house and planning a wedding at the same time. We were moving fast, fast, fast, and that is how I liked it.

Life hasn't slowed down much since then.

Chapter 26
Trouble in Paradise

We were married in what couldn't have been a more perfect ceremony if I had dreamed it. Preacher Van and Pastor Paul officiated over the ceremony. I was so happy, even though many thought it wouldn't last because of my history and how fast we got married, but I knew it would. God sent me this man. I prayed for him and here he is. I knew he was God's plan for me.

After we were married, and lived in an apartment for about six months, we finally moved into our cute little house. I had been so preoccupied with all of the new experiences and changes in my life that I stayed on a "natural high" for over a year. We adopted a dog, Reagan and she was my baby. I spent most of my time decorating the house, shopping with my mom and my sister, working at the church.

When the house was decorated, I immersed myself in ministry at work. Not only was I the administrative assistant for the Pastor, and the church secretary, but Mark and I also started a new ministry called Free Camp. This was an amazing time in my life. The first year, we took 30, nine to twelve year olds, who otherwise would not be able to attend a summer camp to Free Camp for three days. It was held at the denomination's state headquarters. The following years we were blessed to increase the number up to 100 kids.

During those years, we adopted another dog, Hartley. He became my anti-anxiety drug. If I had a bad day, he would cuddle me and it was odd how he had the ability to take away the negativity. He only liked me and Mark. Everyone else, he wanted to kill…or at least it seemed that way. He was very protective of me and still is. But, he created a calm in me that I needed very much.

Around that same time, I took over the Wedding Ministry and Angel Tree Program at the church. I loved serving God in these ways. Finding the humor in God's plan is fun for me. I was an ex-prostitute, married to an ex-cop, and I was the Director of the Wedding Ministry. I guess God really does make you new. For so many years, I thought God was this dead serious, I will smite you God. But, I never considered that He would have such a fabulous sense of humor. We are made in His likeness, so why wouldn't He be funny too?

The Wedding Ministry appealed to me so much that after a couple of years, I branched out on the side and began an event planning business called The Event Gallery of Greenville. I loved it. It was my business, but my family was always there to help. My mother especially. She was with me for every wedding, all day long. We wore each other out. I don't think I had the confidence to do any of it without her support and guidance. It was a fabulous time in my life. I was so busy with everything that I never had a chance to dwell on my past. The present seemed just perfect, but was it really?

Over the years of being so involved at work, with ministry and my new business, I found myself neglecting my husband. I never had time for him, being gone all the time. Some days I would go in to work at 8am and get home at 8pm after meeting with brides or whatever I was involved in at church. Then I was gone all weekend with weddings. He always went to bed early, still does, so I didn't see him most nights for longer than 30 minutes or an hour. This caused a huge strain on our marriage.

Mark is an amazing man, and he puts up with me so very well, but we are very different in one really big way. I wear my emotions on my sleeve and the only thing he got excited about was going fishing. Other than that, no emotion at all. He is "level," never a blip on the screen. I never knew when he was upset, happy, scared, mad or excited. He was a master at hiding his emotions.

I hadn't exactly realized how far apart we had grown until I mentioned to him about wanting to have a child. IVF seemed like a great option, and I just wanted to check into it. After mentioning it to him, he said to me and not in a nice way, "If you want to have children, you will have to do it with someone else."

Total silence. Up until this day, Mark had always been very eager to make me happy. He had even told my mother and father that he would never be able to tell me, "no" about anything.

After the moment of shock passed, I ran crying into the bedroom and my beloved fur babies, Reagan and Hartley came in to console me. They stayed with me for several hours. Mark never came in and I was devastated. The peace I had felt was gone. God had not put it in Mark's heart to have more children and He had not taken the desire out of my heart. I began to doubt that God could handle this one. Maybe I was wrong about trusting God. I wanted so badly to take back my resolve of allowing God to handle this part of my life. I felt confused. Now I know, we were not ready at that time. We had a lot of work to do first.

* * *

I had been so busy with MY life that I hadn't even noticed that OUR life was falling apart. The next 6 months were a roller coaster. We went to marriage counseling and things were iffy for quite a while. I did not want our marriage to fail. We had made promises to each other and to God and I for one did not see divorce as an option. We had both agreed before we were married that divorce would never be an option for us. We would do whatever it took to make it work.

There were some days I didn't feel love for him, but I had to decide to continue to love him. He had to do the same. In marriage, it can be hard to love the other person all the time. You just have to make a decision, sometimes several times a day.

About 3 months into the marriage counseling, Mark received a call about a job opportunity in Northern Virginia. He wasn't sure about going for the interview, but I was ready to get a fresh start. New place, new start, just he and I. I encouraged him to go and interview for the position. We didn't have to decide anything right away. Let's just see if he even gets offered the job. Mark flew out two days later and would return the following day.

When he returned, he had been offered the job. I am so thankful that I can make decisions pretty quickly. Probably a talent I learned on the streets. No time to waste weighing options, decide and move on. He was to start in two weeks. I was game for the move, but we had to sell our home.

Mark suggested that I stay behind until we sold the house and he would go up ahead of me to begin working and live in an apartment until I could come. This was unacceptable to me. It was 2010 and the market had just crashed. It would take a long time to sell the house. In my heart, I knew we had to stay together or all of the things we had been working on would go down the drain. We packed, put our home on the rental market and two weeks later moved into a small apartment in Fredericksburg, VA. The Greens at Falls Run, Luxury Apartments would be our new home for a while and our Greenville home rented quickly by the end of the month.

Chapter 27

The Luxury Apartments

This was the first time since I was delivered from my addictions that I would not have a job and would be at home all day, alone, while Mark was at work. I was a little nervous about it so, I spent quite a bit of time on Facebook connecting with family and friends back home. It made the transition much easier. It honestly didn't feel like I was so far away. Most days I would look out the window of the "luxury apartment" and watch the neighbors coming and going. It wasn't long before I figured out that I had fallen prey to false advertising. "Luxury" was not a word I would have chosen for this particular complex we now lived in.

It is kind of funny now, as I remember it and write about it. One day, I was watching out the double window at the front of the apartment and I see two police cars pull up. Back in the day, this would have completely freaked me out as I hid whatever drugs and paraphernalia I had laying around, but now I had no worries. I just watched. Then I saw the two officers emerge from the 1st floor apartment with a couple of individuals in hand cuffs, being placed in the back seat of each car.

Interesting, wonder what they did?

I posted a bit about it on Facebook and had some conversation about what it could be or not be. Just some interesting banter with my friends to fill my time.

I still hadn't ventured out of the complex on my own. For some reason, I just didn't feel confident in my new city. It kind of concerned me, but I just tried to relax and enjoyed my time off with my dogs at home, watching the world outside through my window.

A few days passed and I looked through my window to the world and I see two gentlemen with baseball bats outside on the other side of the street. There was a row of thick shrubs there and I watched as the fellas stashed the bats in the bushes. WELL, immediately, I knew what was happening and I panicked a little. There was going to be a fight and my car was parked right there across the street. Now, keep in mind that I am pretty street savvy, I lived on the streets in NYC and the Bronx, NY. So, I knew stuff was getting ready to go down and I didn't want my car to be assaulted. Immediately I ran out and moved it. Thinking back on it now, I probably should have called the police first, but I loved my little car and I didn't want anything to happen to it. Afterwards, I called the police. Two more arrests in the books at the "luxury apartments." I am still unsure what they actually arrested them for, but nonetheless, in the back of the car they went.

My new digs now had a name on Facebook, *The Luxury Apartments*. I wrote daily about the goings on at "The Luxury Apartments." It became a joke and it was fun to report the news from my window. However, I knew our time there needed to be short.

The days went by and riding around with Mark at night had helped me with the confidence I needed to leave the apartment and venture out on my own. I went out, signed up at a tanning salon and went directly back to the apartment. It was literally .4 miles from the apartment, but I was getting out. I still didn't realize that this was the beginning of an annoying issue that would be diagnosed a few years down the road.

After working at the church and being so involved in ministry and my business, this down time was a huge struggle for me. I loved feeling so close to God every day and all of a sudden, I felt as if I was separated from Him. That He was not there with me in Fredericksburg. I wanted to go back, to a place where I could almost feel Him, in a tangible way, with me every single day. I needed to feel Him with me. I was safe if He was with me. I began to feel as if I was truly alone. I didn't have God with me and I didn't have heroin with me. I was totally stripped down to just me. At least that is how it felt.

The last straw at *The Luxury Apartments* was the day I woke up to a leak in the bathroom ceiling. We were on the first floor and we were constantly aggravated by the children in the upstairs apartment running back and forth, back and forth, back and forth ALL DAY LONG! It was like a stampede up there and it would go on into the night and start back bright and early.

Don't these people ever go out? Yes, the irony, I know.

I called the maintenance department and they came right out. The leak was right above the tub. They went upstairs and found at least one litter of around two-month-old Pit Bull puppies. The bathtub was filled with water and much had spilt out of the tub. We assumed it was for them to drink.

Well, the renters upstairs did not have a pet agreement and they were breeding Pit Bulls in an apartment, in *The Luxury Apartments*. Being an animal lover, I was ticked off. The puppies quite possibly had never been outside, they were the children running back and forth all day long. They had been cooped up in that apartment their entire lives. Poor babies. Soon, they were all evicted and we didn't have new neighbors upstairs again. It was probably pretty damaged from all the dogs, but who knows.

That was pretty much the last straw. Our plan was to rent for about 6 months and then begin looking for a home to buy. Well, I think we had been in The Luxury Apartments for about 3 months and it was time to go. I couldn't get out of there fast enough. It was not unlike some of the places I had lived in my past and I did not want to be there anymore. It was time to go.

During the two weeks of packing and getting ready to move to Fredericksburg from Greenville, NC, I had done a few online searches for homes in the Northern Virginia area. I had come across a website for a builder who was building in a neighborhood in Fredericksburg, which was as far South of DC as we could go due to Mark's commute. Well, I fell in love with the neighborhood. It was beautiful and WAY out of our price range. But, it was placed in my heart to live in that neighborhood.

Mark, I am sure, was feeling the pressure. I had my heart set on something we clearly could not afford. He told me, "We are not Lovey and Thurston, Honey, we cannot afford to live there." He made it a joke, but I knew he wanted it for me.

So, back in *The Luxury Apartments*, I called a realtor that was showing a house I had found online. I told her I wanted to see that house and that I wanted to move as soon as possible. After explaining all of the happenings to her, she could tell I was ready to get out of there and she made it her business to take me to every house I wanted to see. She never had to send me listings, I found them all on my own. My spirits lifted because I had a job to do again. I finally had something to keep my mind busy. I had a project! Not to mention that one of my favorite past times is looking at real estate and going on open house tours. Almost daily I would have a list of homes I wanted to see and she would take me to them.

Our realtor was amazing. She knew our budget and she carried a calculator with her. I would walk in the house and start rattling off the items that would need to be fixed, updated, or torn out and replaced, while she would calculate estimated costs. If it went much over our budget we would leave and go to the next house. We worked very well together. I liked her a lot and it felt nice to have someone to talk to.

We shared a bit about our lives with each other. I love hearing other people's stories. It gives an endearing quality to the person. I am drawn to people who are open to sharing the closed off parts of their lives with others. For me, it helps me feel closer to them. Sometimes I forget that everybody's lives are not perfect. I look at their lives and see the Norman Rockwell painting and forget that we all have our issues. Knowing their stories helps me to understand why people do the things they do, knowing what their life has experienced.

I was constantly looking at foreclosed homes in my neighborhood of choice. It was 2010, so foreclosures were easy to come by. The home prices were at an all-time low due to the market crash, but we would still be stretching to buy a new home in that neighborhood. Well, one day I found two foreclosed homes in my dream neighborhood. I frantically called Sarah, my Realtor, and she rushed right over and we headed to view the homes. The first one was pretty much destroyed cosmetically. The owners had taken everything out, light fixtures, cabinet knobs, faucets, etc. and they had damaged much of the cabinets and walls. It was a complete overhaul and would be way out of our budget. Not to mention that I need a house that backed to woods or had no backdoor neighbor. My dogs would bark endlessly if there was ever anyone outside and within their sight.

We headed over to the other home, I called Mark and asked him to meet us at the second home. I had viewed some pictures online and I thought it could be the one. Mark met us there and we went inside. It was priced right, backed up to a large hill, no homes back there, but needed some things done in the short term to make it livable. We calculated and re-calculated. We looked all over, up and down and all around. I just knew there was a hidden issue we were overlooking, but we could not find it. I loved it! I jumped up and down and kept saying, "Let's make an offer! Let's make an offer!"

Mark, with his even, no emotion having self, said, "Ok. If this is the one you want."

We went to Sarah's local office and wrote up the offer. I could hardly stand it. I called my parents and asked them to come and see it and for my Dad to look it over and see if he could find the hidden issues it MUST have. They came right up the next day and we went over. I was so excited. I just knew God had lead me to this neighborhood and this home.

My mother was excited for us, but she said, "This is a lot of house for just two people, but it is priced right."

I said, "I think it will be an awesome investment. It is priced really well and when the market comes back we could make a pretty penny on it." All of us agreed, it was a good home, a good investment and a good price. Little did we know what God actually had planned for this house.

Now to wait to hear from Sarah. She warned me that it might take a while since we were dealing with the bank. She also warned of a possible bidding war since it was priced so well. I prayed there would not be a bidding war, but alas, there was. We upped our bid as much as we could and waited some more. My cell rang.

"Mark and Dana? Are you sitting down?"

Chapter 28
A New Home for a New Start

"Oh my gosh, Sarah, tell me. What happened? Did we get the house?" I gushed.

"Yes, you got the house!! We will close at the end of August."

I screamed in excitement. It was a beautiful home in the neighborhood of my dreams and it was big enough for family to come and visit. As a matter of fact, Mark's family and my family could all come and there would be plenty of room for everyone. I could hardly contain myself.

Now, the wait to closing. The paperwork. The anxiety about getting the money. I felt as though I had been on the most drastic of roller coasters in the last few months. I was ready to get off and get back to some form of normalcy. Decorate the house and look for a part time job. But first, we needed to close on our home.

We closed on September 10, 2010 and moved in on September 11. It was a redeeming day for me. On September 11, 2001, I was a totally different person who never even dreamed a day like this one was possible. A drug addicted scam artist, with no foreseeable future. But, this September 11, I was a new person and God was providing a totally new life for me. I was grateful. I felt God blessing us. We had struggled quite a bit before moving to Virginia, but we kept our vows. We worked through it and we continued to work on our marriage.

The next several months were a lot of fun. Decorating was always an interest of mine and I was now developing a love for designing the interior of a home and overseeing contractors. There was a bit of work to be done. It was so much fun and I loved having my mom there with me for a couple of weeks. I dreamed of flipping houses, I thought about how it might become a reality. It hasn't happened yet, but maybe someday.

* * *

We were completely moved into the house, there was still much to be done, but over time we would do it. It came time for me to start looking for a part time job. I began applying and was very conscious of my felony charge, it was like a dark cloud over my head. I was afraid it would prevent me from getting anything decent at all. However, I never lied about it when applying for a job. I would beg for a chance just to be interviewed. If they could just meet with me, they would see that I am a different person than I used to be.

Since working for the church in NC, I loved the idea of working at another church or at a non-profit. Helping people is something I have been passionate about for a long time. There was a job listing in the paper for a local charity. It was a part time job in the accounting department. After emailing my resume', I felt very optimistic. A couple of days later the phone rang and I was offered an interview. I went shopping for a new outfit to wear and I researched the organization online so I would be prepared for the interview.

Pulling up for the interview, I prayed that I wouldn't cry. I always cried at important events in my life, or when talking about myself in any capacity, or singing during worship at church, or when seeing a dead animal on the side of the road. Come to think of it, I cried a lot, about everything. I did not want to cry in this interview, especially like I did when Pastor Paul interviewed me.

"Barb, Dana Brown is here to see you," said the receptionist into the phone. A moment later, "You can go ahead back. Straight down that hall, the door right in front of you." I knocked and thankfully the face I saw was comforting, she was a sweet woman who obviously had her hands full with all of the piles of work on her desk.

The interview was going well, I passed a short test of accounting questions, filled out some paperwork and there was still nothing about criminal history… and I thought, *I better go ahead and tell her about the felony, before I get my hopes up too much.* I told her all about it, crying all the while, and she seemingly shrugged it off. She basically said something to the effect of, I can tell you are no longer that person. She then introduced me to the other woman in our department, then to the boss lady. That was nerve wracking, but she seemed very nice as well. It was looking good.

Once back in Barb's office, she asked, "When can you start?"

"As soon as you need me." I answered.

"Can you start Monday?"

"Yes, I can." I was on top of the world. God was working more miracles. The home, the job, He was opening doors. When God opens a door, no one can shut it. I had never given much thought to Deuteronomy 31:8, which says, "The LORD himself goes before you and will be with you; he will never leave you nor forsake you. Do not be afraid; do not be discouraged." However, I was living out this scripture in my life. He had been going before me for many years and now it was becoming apparent to me. Looking back now, I am amazed at how He went before me and ordered my steps in sync with other's people's steps in order to bring about the desires of my heart. I only pray that He used me in these steps to help others as well.

Throughout the next few months, I began to notice my mental state was coinciding with my ability to make things happen. When I was happy and excited, I was a go getter. When I was feeling anxious and sad, I could not function very well and cried at the drop of a hat. Barb noticed this in me and called me to her office.

She began to share with me about her own life and how she saw similarities in me. She asked if I minded her talking to me about my feelings. I said I didn't mind. I have always been an open book. So, she shared with me her need for an antidepressant and how it had helped her to level her mood so she could function normally. She thought maybe I should discuss with my doctor about depression and see if it could help me as well. Within the month, I was taking an antidepressant and a couple of weeks later I was feeling so much better. My depression and anxiety were both gone. I felt confident again and ready to live life to the fullest. This included revisiting my dream of becoming a mother.

The organization I worked for was run by women and the employees were all women most of the time. We occasionally had a man come in but they didn't stay long. I can't for the life of me imagine why they didn't stick around. Anyway, I had become friends with a few of the women there. I began to share my desire to become a mother with one woman in particular, Tam, who is also a follower of Christ. She promised to pray for God to grant me the desires of my heart.

Chapter 29

The Desires of My Heart

I had been on the job for almost a year. Mentally, the most stable I had been in my entire life. It was obvious to me now, that all of the drugs and alcohol in my past were an unconscious effort to self-medicate the depression and anxiety I had suffered all along. The complete obsession with staying busy with work and ministry were another means of self-medicating. But now, my husband and I were healthier and happier than we had been our entire marriage. God was bringing me to a place of contentment. There was still that desire to be a mom, but I was content in this place. Life finally felt good.

The employment door was a fast revolving one at the organization and people came and went. I can't even remember all the new hires who left as fast as they came in. One day, a beautiful blonde was hired. She was smart and friendly and a little sassy. I liked her. She was funny and we could chat about this and that during breaks. Her name was Lucy. Lucy, Tam, Pat and I could talk openly with each other and know that it was confidential. There was quite a bit of unhappiness at the organization and we could vent to one another. Tam and Pat were praying for another job, and I would join in praying for God to open doors for them. Tam and I would talk about the fact that God had us all there, at that organization, for a reason. In His time, He would reveal His plan for each of us. Tam vowed to be a light to others while she was there. And she was.

* * *

Christmas 2011, I started feeling this desire to be a mother stronger than ever, but I was still content with life. Planning for Christmas and gift buying, decorating for Christmas was consuming much of my time off from work. One day, I saw a commercial for a show called *A Home for the Holidays.* It is an annual program focused on finding families for foster children who would love a family and they are basically presenting their case on TV. I recorded the show to watch later.

A few days later, I began to watch the program about 30 minutes before Mark came home from work. All of a sudden, I had a brilliant idea... ok, well a sneaky idea. I decided to wait until Mark walked in the door to continue to watch the program and maybe he would watch it with me. He is a softy and maybe it would pull his heartstrings and he would be open to discussing adoption.

It worked. He watched it with me. After the show was over, he quietly went upstairs. I thought, well, maybe he will think about it a little. When he came back down he said to me, "This house is too big and empty, let's get some kids in it."

"REALLY?!? Are you sure? I mean, really??" I squealed.

"Yes, I am sure." in his even, non-emotional way, he was

ready. My sister was right. God had placed the desire for children in his heart instead of taking it out of mine. Albeit, I used a deceptive trick to get him to watch that program, God used it despite myself. I was online researching different adoption options within minutes.

* * *

Back at work on Monday, I shared my new project with my friends. They were so excited for me. I had researched myself into complete confusion over the weekend. I had no idea what to do, how to do it or if my past would hinder our plans. Thankfully, trusting God, and my new medications, were both helping to keep the anxiety at bay.

Buzz, my phone rang from Lucy's office. I answered and she said, "Ya know, my mom works for DSS and you should contact her about fostering to adopt."

All of a sudden, the plan was clear. Social Services and foster children was the direction God wanted us to go. I am amazed at how God lines up our lives with the lives of others, and if we just wait on Him, He will take care of everything. He placed Lucy in my life at that time to lead us to the right option for us. We began Foster Parent Training in February of 2012. We completed in May and were approved to be foster parents. My history was not going to hinder us. I was so excited and nervous. I was ready for kids. Like NOW. At least once a week, I would call Lucy's mother, Amy, to ask if any children had come in.

"Any kids? We are ready. Call us for anyone." I would say. Mark and I had decided we would say yes to any call that we received. If God was putting us in that child's path, then that child or those children were the ones He wants us to have. That is exactly what we did.

The first call was for a sibling group of five children. Fourteen-year-old twins, a 10, 6 and 5-year-old, the youngest with cerebral palsy. It was suggested that they would place three with us and two with another family. I immediately called Mark and told him their plan.

"Why are they gonna separate them? Tell them we will take them all."

Mark is a soft-hearted man. He wanted them to stay together. We had the space to do it, so I called them back and told them we wanted them…all of them. The weekend was spent shopping and praying for these children. Already feeling very protective over them, especially the five-year-old because he had CP, I was feeling like Mama Bear.

They were to arrive Monday around 3pm. I went to work Monday morning and posted a picture on my office door of a stork with five babies, in appropriately colored blankets, hanging from his beak. It was so cute. Everyone saw it and came in to congratulate me, however they all responded with "FIVE?" I was over the moon, a little nervous to meet them, but completely confident in our ability to care for these children.

I was preparing to leave work at 2pm when my phone rang. It was Amy, "Dana, I am so sorry, but an aunt stepped up to take the children. It is always better for them to stay with family if at all possible." She stayed on the phone with me for a few minutes to make sure I was ok. I was not ok. I felt as if I had just lost a pregnancy, broken hearted. However, I wanted what was best for these five children I already loved and never got to meet.

I called Mark and shared the news. He was calm and said, "They weren't our kids." Once at home, I began to fall apart. Mark said, "This is why I was unsure about this, I don't want to see you upset all the time."

Sniffling, I responded, "Just let me go upstairs and cry for a bit and I will be fine." That is what I did and I was fine. I was ready for the next call.

It had been about three months since we were officially approved to be foster parents and the first call fell through, as well as the second and third. I am grateful that I never got a chance to see the children because I know it would have been so much more difficult. They had all found a better fit for their lives and like Mark said, "they weren't our kids." They were not the kids God had for us and we weren't the parents God had for them.

In August of 2012 I got a call about a 14-year-old girl who had been placed in several foster homes. None had worked out and she needed a new home. Mark was out of town on business, but DSS wanted me to do a weekend respite where we could meet each other. I was a nervous wreck to meet her by myself, but I said it was fine. I thought, *we can do girl stuff.* I planned nails and shopping.

Alyssa came to the door with her social worker, she was pretty, had blonde hair and green eyes. I realized then that fourteen looks a lot different than it did when I was fourteen. I would have passed her for seventeen at least. She was quiet and I was amazed at her ability to go in to a stranger's house and look so comfortable. We had a good weekend together.

Mark called after the weekend was over and we discussed Alyssa. I said, "I like her. We told God we would say yes." And so, we did, we told DSS we would foster her either until she went back to her biological family or aged out or we would adopt her if she wanted us to. It would be up to her. DSS was skeptical, they had heard this before with many kids. Most times they were bounced around despite the promises of foster homes. Alyssa would move in at our home the following weekend.

I introduced Alyssa to Mark and the first words I believe Mark told her were, "You don't ever have to move again, unless you want to. You can be here as long as you like." He meant it and for the next year she tested his resolve.

That very weekend that Alyssa moved in, we got a call from DSS about a three-year-old girl and a five-year-old boy who also needed to change foster homes. They were siblings and available to adopt. We still had room and Alyssa was older so I thought we could handle it. We said yes again. This social worker was not completely forthcoming of the issues that would confront us with these siblings. I guess I should be thankful, because we may have gone back on our promise to say yes.

The next weekend we met "The Littles." That is what we call them when discussing them as a pair. They love it. That day, the doorbell rang and I opened the door to the most beautiful, bright, nervous little faces I had ever seen.

The three-year-old stuck her chubby, little hand out to shake mine and said, "Hello, Mrs. Brown, my name is Jaden." I giggled at her little tiny, growny self. She was small for a three-year-old and I was immediately smitten. She was the cutest thing…no seriously, she was. I remember thinking, *She is going to be a handful.* So far, there has never been a more prophetic thought to cross my mind.

Then Lance, who was much quieter, said, "Hewwo, my name is Wance." I melted into a puddle of "you can have whatever you want from me." He was to be my absolutely precious, extremely caring, totally handsome son. He would be the strong, silent type, I just know it. He has since proved me right in my evaluation. He is my little gentleman and so sensitive and sweet. Back off girls…it will be YEARS before I am ready to let him go.

The next year, however, was proving to be so very difficult. There were many ups and downs and doubts about our abilities to parent these children and doubts that we had really followed God's plan. Transitions for foster children are very difficult and traumatic, not to mention the trauma they suffered before they came to us, in their own homes by the very people who were supposed to protect them. That in itself was one huge struggle, but our experience with one particular social worker was not easy and sometimes was ridiculously, unnecessarily burdensome. However, we told God we would say yes and we would not give up. It seemed this woman had a plan to destroy our placement...or the kids in general. So, we didn't give up. He blessed us and strengthened us. It is amazing to look back on it with a knowledge that God got us through that year, because there is no way we could have without Him.

One year from the time they arrived at our home, in September of 2013, all three were officially adopted. During that year, I became a stay at home mom. We all needed the time to adjust. Life has been amazing and tough and wonderfully hard and full of love and laughter and screaming fits. I don't have the screaming fits as often anymore. None of us would change any of it for the world. Currently, I am homeschooling The Littles and loving every minute of being Mommy to these amazing children. Alyssa is a senior in high school and we look forward to supporting her in whatever life has in store for her. She is an amazingly strong, bold, hard headed, and beautiful young woman, with a lot to learn about how beautiful life is and should be. Maybe one day they will want to share their own stories. I will encourage that, because it has been completely cathartic for me, and I have no doubt it will be for them as well. They are so very inspiring! All of them. I can't wait to see how God will use them. I know it will be in BIG ways!

Afterword

My sister Selena's prayer for me during the years I was so very lost, taken from her prayer journal:

"Lord, Dana is a huge burden on my heart. I would love to see her on fire for You. Her salvation is my strongest desire in this life. I love her and want her to see the value of her soul."

If someone you love is represented in any of these chapters, I urge you to pray for them. Do not give up hope, for with God all things are possible. I have been told by some of the people who prayed for me during that time that they were "praying against hope." They didn't think there was any hope for me or that I would even live much longer, but they kept praying. So, you keep praying too.

If you are reading this book and you see yourself in these chapters and you know your life is spiraling out of control, ask Jesus to come into your life. Ask Him to become your Lord and Savior, then you follow His lead. It is just that simple. He is ready to heal your hurts and to forgive anything you may have done. I mean, wipe it clean. A new start. Your life may or may not immediately turn around, but it is the first step, you must take the next steps in faith, that God loves you and has an amazing plan for your life.

Contact me at **desperateforafix@gmail.com** and let me know you have made this life changing decision. I will be happy to answer any questions and point you in the direction of a loving, nurturing church to call or visit in your city.

We will always have ups and downs, but seriously, with Christ, there is this amazing peace you can have and a promise that He will never leave you or forsake you. Being a child of God comes with the knowledge that He will provide for you and His strength can get you through anything. Get ready for the best life you can have!